S0-BFS-041

English Reading Comprehension
For the Spanish Speaker

Book 4

For Ages 10 - Adult

RETURN TO
ADULT LITERACY
OFFICE

Written by
Kathleen Fisher

Illustrated by
Kathleen Duncan & Paul Widosh

Fisher Hill   Huntington Beach   California

NOTICE! Copies of worksheets may be reproduced by the classroom teacher for classroom use only. Reproduction of these materials for an entire school or school system is strictly prohibited.

Copyright 2008 by Kathleen Fisher
All rights reserved.

Published by FISHER HILL
5267 Warner Avenue, #166
Huntington Beach, CA 92649-4079

Made in the U.S.A.

Publisher's Cataloging in Publication

Fisher, Kathleen S., 1952-
    English reading comprehension for the Spanish speaker.
Book 1 / by Kathleen Fisher. --1st ed.
        p. cm.
        Audience: Ages 10-adult.
        Includes bibliographical references and index.
        ISBN 13: 978-1-878253-47-7

        1. English language--Textbooks for foreign speakers--
Spanish. 2. English as a second language.

Table of Contents

Contenido

Introduction

The purpose of this book is to help Spanish speakers improve their English reading comprehension skills. Reading comprehension is the ability to draw meaning from written words. This is an excellent book to use after finishing *English Reading Comprehension for The Spanish Speaker Book 3* and *English Reading and Spelling for the Spanish Speaker Book 4*.

This book is made up of twenty lessons. Lessons include practice with fluency, vocabulary, comprehension, phonics and phonology. There is an answer key at the end of each lesson.

Reading smoothly (fluency) is an important skill. Fluency allows readers to think about what they are reading instead of having to think about sounding out words. Decoding skills need to be learned and practiced so these skills become automatic when reading words. Visualizing (making pictures in your head) helps readers remember what they have read. Good vocabulary skills help readers visualize. Readers can not visualize a word if they do not know its meaning. All of these skills: fluency, visualizing, vocabulary, and decoding are necessary to have good reading comprehension.

Reading comprehension is the goal of reading. Reading is an essential skill for jobs and daily life. Many people enjoy reading and say it is one of their favorite pastimes. Others read only when it is necessary. Whichever the case may be, everyone needs to know how to read. Learning to read comes easier to some people. Most people need to be taught how to read. It is different than learning to talk. For some people, learning to read can be very difficult but with practice, most people can learn to read.

Introducción

Comprensión de lectura en inglés para hispanohablantes Libro 4 se escribió para ayudar a quienes hablan español a mejorar su habilidad de comprensión de la lectura en inglés. La comprensión de la lectura es la facultad de extraer significado de las palabras escritas. Este es un libro excelente para usarse después de terminar *Comprensión de lectura en inglés para hispanohablantes Libro 3* y *Lectura y escritura en inglés para hispanohablantes Libro 4*.

Este libro está compuesto de veinte lecciones. Las lecciones incluyen la práctica de las habilidades de fluidez, vocabulario, comprensión y decodificación. Hay una clave de respuestas al final de cada lección.

El leer sin interrupciones (la fluidez) es una habilidad importante. La fluidez permite a los lectores pensar lo que están leyendo en lugar de tener que pensar en pronunciar las palabras. Las habilidades de decodificación deben aprenderse y practicarse para que estas habilidades se hagan automáticas cuando se leen las palabras. La visualización (formar imágenes en su cabeza) ayuda a los lectores a recordar lo que han leído. Las habilidades del buen vocabulario ayudan a los lectores a visualizar. Los lectores no pueden visualizar una palabra si no saben lo que significa. Todas estas habilidades: la fluidez, la visualización, el vocabulario y la decodificación son necesarias para tener una buena comprensión de la lectura.

La comprensión de la lectura es la meta de la lectura. Leer es una habilidad esencial para los empleos y la vida diaria. Mucha gente disfruta de la lectura y dice que es uno de sus pasatiempos favoritos. Otros leen sólo cuando es necesario. Cualquiera que sea el caso, todos necesitan saber cómo leer. El aprender a leer es más fácil para algunas personas. La mayoría de las personas necesitan que se les enseñe cómo leer. Es diferente que aprender a hablar. Para algunas personas, aprender a leer puede ser algo muy difícil, pero con práctica, casi todos pueden aprender a leer.

Lesson 1 * Lección 1

Vocabulary * Vocabulario

Animals * Animales

bird
ave

squirrel
ardilla

bull
toro

shrimp
camarón

squid
calamar

turtle
tortuga

tiger
tigre

lion
león

kangaroo
canguro

zebra
cebra

feather
pluma

fur
piel

Fill in the Blanks * Llene el Espacio

Llene cada espacio con una palabra de la página de vocabulario. Use la figura al final de la oración para ayudarse. Lea la oración con cuidado porque puede necesitar añadir una <u>s</u> o las letras <u>es</u> a la palabra del vocabulario.

1. Look at the peacock spread its bright tail _feather_ .

2. We saw six _lions_ on our vacation to Africa.

3. The _Kangaroo_ has a joey in its pouch.

4. Be careful. There is a _bull_ in the pasture.

5. The _turtle_ has a shell for protection.

6. Mammals have _fur_ and birds have feathers.

7. Take a picture of the _tiger_ sleeping in the tree.

8. The _birds_ were taking a bath in the puddle.

9. _Zebras_ have black and white stripes.

10. My father caught a _squid_ with his harpoon.

11. Look at the _squirrel_ with the big bushy tail eating an acorn on top of the large concrete block.

12. For dinner the boy ate six pieces of _shrimp_ .

2

Sea Turtles

Did you know sea turtles have been around since the dinosaurs? Now, after existing for over 100 million years, sea turtles are struggling to survive! Unfortunately, threats like hunting, habitat destruction, and pollution have wiped out entire turtle populations. Today three of the seven existing species are endangered with extinction. What can people do to help the sea turtles?

In Mexico, children help baby sea turtles reach the Pacific Ocean. On a special day, children come to the beach to release baby sea turtles into the ocean. They hold the turtles then gently release them into the ocean. Where do children get these sea turtles and why does Mexico have this special day?

Female sea turtles return to the same beach where they were born to lay their eggs. Turtle eggs are the size of ping-pong balls. It will take the eggs 50-60 days to hatch. When the baby turtles hatch, it can take them up to two days to dig their way up to the top of their nest. If the baby turtles feel warm sand, they will stop digging until the sand cools down which means the sun has set and it is nighttime. The baby turtles want to make their journey to the ocean at night so the sun will not dry them out and there will be fewer predators. After the turtles burst out of the sand, they head for the brightest area which is usually the ocean where the moon's reflection is shining brightly. Sometimes the baby sea turtles will get confused if there are condos and hotels with bright lights. Then the baby turtles may walk in the wrong direction. Every year baby turtles are killed crossing roads and getting dried out.

In Mexico, naturalists dig up turtle eggs and keep them safe until they hatch. It's easy to find a sea turtle's nest because the mother turtle leaves a large track from the ocean to the nest. When the baby sea turtles are ready, children return the babies to the ocean. Hopefully, this day gives children and their parents an awareness of the importance of sea turtles in the marine and beach/dune ecosystems.

Is it possible that a world in which sea turtles cannot survive may soon become a world in which humans struggle to survive? Species have been going extinct for millions of years; it is a natural part of the evolutionary process. Today, however, species are going extinct because of abrupt changes brought about by humans. Habitat destruction, pollution, and over consumption are causing species to decline at a rate never before seen in history. Many people are trying to save the sea turtles by volunteering or donating money to conservation and research groups. They want to save these majestic sea creatures that have inhabited the oceans for over 10 million years.

Comprehension Questions

Use la información en *Sea Turtles* para contestar las siguientes preguntas. Conteste cada pregunta con una oración completa.

1. How many years have sea turtles been on earth?

   _____

2. How many species of sea turtles are there?

   _____

3. How many are endangered?

   _____

4. What does endangered mean?

   _____

5. Why are sea turtles struggling to survive?

   _____

6. Poaching has a similar meaning to hunting, pollution, or habitat destruction?

   _____

7. Where do sea turtles lay their eggs?

   _____

8. Why do baby sea turtles wait until nighttime to make their journey to the ocean?

   _____

9. Name two ways people are helping the sea turtles?

   _____

10. Write one fact you learned from *Sea Turtles*?

    _____

Prefixes * Prefijos

Un prefijo es un grupo de letras que se añaden al principio de una palabra para cambiar su significado. En esta página usaremos los siguientes prefijos: <u>in</u>, <u>re</u>, <u>un</u>. Los prefijos <u>in</u> y <u>un</u> significan *no*. El prefijo <u>re</u> significa *otra vez*.

Escriba el significado de cada una de las siguientes palabras. La primera ya está hecha.

1. **unlock**
   not locked

2. **inexpensive**
   _____

3. **inactive**
   _____

4. **unsafe**
   _____

5. **unsaid**
   _____

6. **reheat**
   _____

7. **indirect**
   _____

8. **review**
   _____

9. **refill**
   _____

10. **retrace**
   _____

Complete cada oración con una de las palabras anteriores.

11. We will ____retrace____ our steps through the woods.

12. You need to ____review____ your notes before the test.

13. My mom will ____refill____ our glasses with milk.

14. It is best to leave some thoughts ____unsaid____.

15. Please ____unlock____ the door for your sister.

16. Father will ____reheat____ the leftovers for dinner.

17. Scuba diving alone is ____unsafe____.

18. That store has very ____inexpensive____ clothes.

Homophones * Homófonos

Los homófonos son palabras que suenan de manera similar, pero se escriben de manera diferente y tienen diferentes significados.

Encima de cada oración hay dos homófonos. Elija el correcto para cada oración.

1. tide or tied
   We walked on the beach at low _____ .

2. creak or creek
   We set up our tent near the _____ .

3. peace or piece
   She had a feeling of _____ after helping out at the church.

4. pair or pear
   My brother will buy a new _____ of shoes on Saturday.

5. pain or pane
   The baseball crashed through the window _____ .

6. hire or higher
   The shop needs to _____ five people to repair computers.

7. bear or bare
   In the winter, many trees are _____ .

8. mane or main
   The lion's _____ was full of thistles.

9. tale or tail
   The grandmother told the children a _____ from long ago.

10. sore or soar
   You need to have a doctor check the _____ on your leg.

6

Answer Key * Las Respuestas

Fill in the Blanks * Llene el Espacio (page 2)

1. feathers
2. lions
3. kangaroo
4. bull
5. turtle
6. fur
7. tiger
8. birds
9. zebras
10. squid
11. squirrel
12. shrimp

Comprehension * Comprensión (page 4)

1. Sea turtles have been on earth for over 100 million years.
2. There are seven species of sea turtles.
3. Three of the seven species of sea turtles are endangered.
4. Endangered means the sea turtles may become extinct.
5. The sea turtles are threatened by hunting, habitat destruction and pollution.
6. Poaching is similar to hunting.
7. Female turtles lay their eggs on the same beach where they were born.
8. During the night, the sun will not dry them out and there are fewer predators.
9. The naturalists dig up turtle eggs and keep them safe until they hatch. Children return the baby turtles to the ocean.
10. Many people are trying to save the majestic sea turtles.

Prefixes * Prefijos (page 5)

1.	not locked	10.	trace again
2.	not expensive	11.	retrace
3.	not active	12.	review
4.	not safe	13.	refill
5.	not said	14.	unsaid
6.	heat again	15.	unlock
7.	not direct	16.	reheat
8.	view again	17.	unsafe
9.	fill again	18.	inexpensive

Homophones * Homófonos (page 6)

1.	tide	6.	hire
2.	creek	7.	bare
3.	peace	8.	mane
4.	pair	9.	tale
5.	pane	10.	sore

Lesson 2 * Lección 2

Vocabulary * Vocabulario

People * Personas

girl
niña

boys
niños

people
personas

army
ejército

nurse
enfermera

doctor
doctor

mother
madre

father
padre

aunt
tía

woman
mujer

women
mujeres

uncle
tío

Fill in the Blanks * Llene el Espacio

Llene cada espacio con una palabra de la página de vocabulario. Use la figura al final de la oración para ayudarse. Lea la oración con cuidado porque puede necesitar añadir una <u>s</u> o las letras <u>es</u> a la palabra del vocabulario.

1. The _____ will give you medicine for the infection.

2. The _____ are wearing long dresses to the party.

3. My _____ has had a cough for two weeks.

4. Many _____ work for the electric company.

5. In the _____, she worked as an electrician.

6. My _____ has an enormous bump on his head!

7. My _____ felt nervous when she saw the boys high up in the trees.

8. The _____ will entertain us with her music.

9. The _____ with the broken leg has to walk with crutches.

10. Once a week the _____ visits the homeless shelter.

11. My _____ scraped her leg when she fell on the pavement.

12. The _____ are wearing yellow shirts.

9

Archie Carr

Do you known someone who is passionate about what he or she does? Fortunately, many of these people help others, care about animals, or are concerned about the environment. Archie Carr was one of these people. He had a keen interest in sea turtles.

Archie Carr has been called the father of sea turtle research. When Dr. Carr died in 1987, sea turtles lost their greatest friend and advocate. He was a biology professor at the University of Florida, author of many papers and books, a lecturer, and an expert on sea turtles, especially the green turtle. For over thirty years, Archie Carr tagged turtles in order to understand their migratory habits. He started a program called "Operation Green Turtle" to re-establish rookeries in places known to have had nesting activity. He helped save the green turtle from destruction in the western Caribbean and inspired others to follow his example. In 1959, Dr. Carr helped found the Caribbean Conservation Corporation dedicated to protecting sea turtles through research, education, advocacy and protection of their habitats. It is the oldest sea turtle research and conservation group in the world.

Dr. Carr was especially interested in the green turtles. There are six other sea turtle species. They are loggerhead, leatherback, hawksbill, Kemp's ridley, olive ridley, and flatback.

Why are sea turtles important? Sea turtles eat sea grass. Sea grass needs to be constantly cut short to be healthy and help it grow across the sea floor. Sea turtles and manatees act as grazing animals that cut the grass short and help maintain the health of the sea grass beds. Over the past decades, there has been a decline in sea grass beds. This decline may be linked to the lower numbers of sea turtles. Sea grass beds are important because they provide breeding and developmental grounds for many species of fish, shellfish and crustaceans. Without sea grass beds, many marine species humans eat would be lost, as would the lower levels of the food chain. The reactions could result in many more marine species being lost and eventually impacting humans.

Archie Carr's enthusiastic support has helped save the sea turtles from extinction. He has inspired others to continue his work to save these magnificent creatures.

Comprehension Questions

Use la información en *Archie Carr* para contestar las siguientes preguntas. Conteste cada pregunta con una oración completa.

1. What was Archie Carr passionate about?

   _____

2. Why has Archie Carr been called the father of sea turtle research?

   _____

3. What is the Caribbean Conservation Corporation?

   _____

4. How many sea turtle species are there?

   _____

5. What does migratory mean?

   _____

6. What are rookeries?

   _____

7. Tell one reason why sea turtles are important?

   _____

8. Give one example of a shellfish.

   _____

9. Give one example of a crustacean.

   _____

10. What does extinction mean?

   _____

Prefixes * Prefijos

Un prefijo es un grupo de letras que se añaden al principio de una palabra para cambiar su significado. En esta página usaremos los siguientes prefijos: dis, im, non. Los prefijos <u>dis</u> y <u>im</u> significan *opuesto*. El prefijo <u>non</u> significa *no* o *sin*.

Escriba el significado de cada una de las siguientes palabras. La primera ya está hecha.

disconnect

1. <s>disconnet</s>
   opposite of connect

2. immature
   _____

3. nonliving
   _____

4. nonpoisonous
   _____

5. impossible
   _____

6. impatient
   _____

7. nonfat
   _____

8. discover
   _____

9. impractical
   _____

10. disappear
   _____

Complete cada oración con una de las palabras anteriores.

11. **A chair is** _____ .

12. **It is** ___9___ **to have white carpet in a house with many children.**

13. **It is** ___5___ **to put that enormous bottle in that box!**

14. **The magician will make the rabbit** ___10___ .

15. **The miners** ___8___ **gold in the creek.**

16. **The electrician will** ___1___ **the wires.**

17. **We saw a** _____ **snake when we were hiking.**

18. **My mom drinks** ___7___ **milk.**

12

Multiple Meanings
Palabras con múltiples significados

Muchas palabras tienen varios significados populares. Escriba dos oraciones por cada palabra asegurándose de que cada oración use un significado diferente de la palabra.

1. mold *moho / molde*

_____

_____

2. pupils *alumnos / pupilos ojos*

_____

_____

3. racket *raqueta / estafa*

_____

_____

4. seal *Foca de mar / To seal cerrar*

_____

_____

5. cast *votar / Yeso*

_____

_____

6. jam *mermelada / enredo*

_____

_____

Answer Key * Las Respuestas

Fill in the Blanks * Llene el Espacio (page 9)

1. doctor
2. women
3. uncle
4. people
5. army
6. father
7. aunt
8. woman
9. girl
10. nurse
11. mother
12. boys

Comprehension * Comprensión (page 11)

1. Archie Carr was passionate about sea turtles.
2. He was an author, lecturer, and expert on sea turtles.
3. The Caribbean Conservation Corporation is dedicated to protecting sea turtles.
4. There are 7 sea turtle species.
5. Migratory means to move from one place to another.
6. Rookeries are places where the sea turtles nest.
7. Sea turtles eat sea grass.
8. A clam is a shell fish.
9. A lobster is a crustacean.
10. Extinction means to have died out or to be gone forever.

Prefixes * Prefijos (page 12)

1.	opposite of connect	10.	opposite of appear
2.	opposite of mature	11.	nonliving
3.	not living	12.	impractical
4.	not poisonous	13.	impossible
5.	opposite of possible	14.	disappear
6.	opposite of patient	15.	discovered
7.	no fat	16.	disconnect
8.	opposite of cover	17.	nonpoisonous
9.	opposite of practical	18.	nonfat

Multiple Meanings * Palabras con múltiples significados (page 13)
Answers will vary. Here are some examples.

1. He poured the plaster into a mold.
   There is mold growing on the bread.
2. There are ten pupils in the class.
   The pupil is a part of the eye.
3. She has her tennis racket in her bag.
   The children are making a loud racket.
4. The seal is resting on the rock.
   The envelope is closed with a seal.
5. The cast of the play did a wonderful job.
   Her broken arm is in a cast.
6. I like strawberry jam on my toast.
   He had to jam on his brakes.

Lesson 3 * Lección 3

Vocabulary * Vocabulario

Places * Lugares

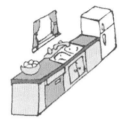

kitchen
cocina

jungle
selva

apartment
apartamento

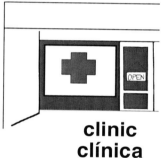

clinic
clínica

forest
bosque

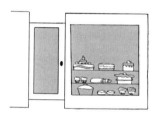

bakery
panadería

ocean
océano

hospital
hospital

mountain
montaña

grocery store
tienda de comestibles

desert
desierto

Earth
Tierra

Fill in the Blanks * Llene el Espacio

Llene cada espacio con una palabra de la página de vocabulario. Use la figura al final de la oración para ayudarse. Lea la oración con cuidado porque puede necesitar añadir una <u>s</u> o las letras <u>es</u> a la palabra del vocabulario.

1. There is more water than land on _____ .

2. He burned his finger in the _____ .

3. On Thursday, we will go hiking in the _____ .

4. My sister went to the _____ to get stitches.

5. The _____ , with its many trees, is home for countless creatures.

6. My brothers like to go fishing in the _____ .

7. My friend's _____ is on the third floor.

8. The _____ on the corner sells enormous pastries.

9. Every Saturday my dad goes to the _____ .

10. When you hike in the _____ you need lots of water.

11. In the _____ we will probably see monkeys.

12. Mom will get her flu shot at the _____ .

16

Channel Islands National Park

Dolphins jumping in pairs, as they surf the wake of your boat is what you might see when you travel to the Channel Islands National Park. These five islands are part of a chain of eight islands located in the Pacific Ocean off the coast of Southern California. San Miguel, Santa Rosa, Santa Cruz, Anacapa, and Santa Barbara islands were made into the Channel Islands National Park in 1980. The Channel Islands National Marine Sanctuary encompasses the waters around the islands. The Channel Islands National Park helps preserve a place where visitors can go to experience coastal southern California as it once was.

The trip from Ventura to Santa Cruz Island takes about an hour by boat. Along the way you may see pods of dolphins. If you're lucky, you may see migrating whales. Once you reach the island, there is a small dock where you will disembark. A ranger may be there to meet and tell you about the island. There are no restaurants so you will need to pack a lunch. There are no trashcans so you will need to pack out all of your trash. What can you do on the island? You can kayak, snorkel, scuba, hike, camp, or just relax. Many people like to kayak because there are caves you can explore and many animals to see. As you kayak, you will see many pelicans and probably several sea lions. The water is crystal clear so you can see colorful fish and purple sea urchins as your kayak skims over large kelp beds. If you decide to hike, you won't encounter may people on the trails. September and October are the best times to visit the island because the weather is warm and sunny. But don't miss the boat for the return trip to the mainland; otherwise, you will have to spend the night and there are no hotels.

Santa Cruz is the largest of the five islands in the Channel Islands National Park. It is 60,645 acres. The smallest of the five islands is the Santa Barbara Island with 639 acres. On all of the islands, you can hike and camp. On several, you can also snorkel, scuba, and kayak. On all of them, you will see wildlife.

The Chumash Indians inhabited the islands for thousands of years. They developed a rich culture dependent on the resources of the land and the sea for survival. By the nineteenth century, there were sheep and cattle ranches on Santa Cruz, Santa Rosa, and San Miguel islands. When you visit the islands today, you can see the remains of the ancient Chumash villages, the historic sheep and cattle ranches, and military structures that have also occupied these islands.

Maybe someday you will have a chance to visit the Channel Islands National Park. What will you want to do there? Have a picnic on the beach, kayak, hike, scuba, or snorkel? Maybe, you'll just want to relax and enjoy the peace and quiet of nature.

Comprehension Questions

Use la información en *Cannel Islands Nathional Park* para contestar las siguientes preguntas. Conteste cada pregunta con una oración completa.

1. Where is the Channel Islands National Park?

   _____

2. How many islands make up the park?

   _____

3. Name three animals you would find in a marine sanctuary.

   _____

4. Name three things you can do at the islands.

   _____

5. What was the name of the Native Americans that lived on the islands.

   _____

6. What is a group of dolphins called?

   _____

7. Name two mammals you may see on your way to the islands.

   _____

8. What is the name of the largest island?

   _____

9. Catalina Island is one of the eight Channel Islands. It is a developed island with hotels, restaurants, homes, shops, and a golf course. Would you <u>rather</u> visit Catalina Island or Santa Cruz Island? Give three reasons for your answer.

   _____

   _____

   _____

Prefixes * Prefijos

Un prefijo es un grupo de letras que se añaden al principio de una palabra para cambiar su significado. En esta página usaremos los siguientes prefijos: <u>mis-</u>, <u>pre-</u>, <u>under-</u>. El prefijo <u>mis-</u> significa *equivocadamente*. El prefijo <u>pre-</u> significa *antes*. El prefijo <u>under-</u> significa *debajo* o *menos que*.

Escriba el significado de cada una de las siguientes palabras. La primera ya está hecha.

1. **underline**
   line below

2. **preheat**
   _____

3. **misplace**
   _____

4. **prepay**
   _____

5. **underground**
   _____

6. **presort**
   _____

7. **undershirt**
   _____

8. **misspelled**
   _____

9. **preview**
   _____

10. **misunderstood**
    _____

Complete cada oración con una de las palabras anteriores.

11. **He will wear an** _____ **to keep warm.**

12. **The subway runs** _____ .

13. **My two sons always** _____ **their keys.**

14. **Let's** _____ **the chapter in science before we read it.**

15. **Please** _____ **the correct answer.**

16. **You need to** _____ **the oven for ten minutes.**

17. **She** _____ **five words on the test.**

18. **The student** _____ **the question.**

Antonyms * Antónimos

Escriba, junto a cada palabra, la palabra que signifique lo contrario o casi lo contrario. Use las palabras de la casilla para contestar.

light	1. _____	(11) full	
left	2. _____	(5) sell	
pretty	3. _____	(12) lose	
awake	4. _____	(13) vanish	
buy	5. _____	(1) right	
present	6. _____	(14) begin	
indoors	7. _____	(10) bright	
crooked	8. _____	(6) absent	
common	9. _____	(15) fat	
gloomy	10. _____	(8) hard	
hungry	11. _____	(4) asleep	
locate	12. _____	(16) minimum	
appear	13. _____	(9) rare	
quit	14. _____	(1) heavy	
slender	15. _____	(17) victory	
maximum	16. _____	(8) straight	
defeat	17. _____	(3) ugly	
easy	18. _____	(7) outdoors	

Answer Key * Las Respuestas

Fill in the Blanks * Llene el Espacio (page 16)

1. earth
2. kitchen
3. mountains
4. hospital
5. forest
6. ocean
7. apartment
8. bakery
9. grocery store
10. desert
11. jungle
12. clinic

Comprehension * Comprensión (page 18)

1. The Park is located in the Pacific Ocean off the coast of Southern California.
2. Five islands make up the park.
3. You might see dolphins, pelicans, and sea lions.
4. At the islands, you can kayak, snorkel, and hike.
5. The Chumash Indians lived on the islands for many years.
6. A group of dolphins is called a pod.
7. You might see dolphins or whales on the way to the islands.
8. The largest island is Santa Cruz.
9. I would rather visit Santa Cruz Island because I like to hike, camp, and relax where there are not many people.

Prefixes * Prefijos (page 19)

1. line below	7. below shirt	13. misplace
2. heat before	8. spelled incorrectly	14. preview
3. place wrongly	9. view before	15. underline
4. pay before	10. understood incorrectly	16. preheat
5. below ground	11. undershirt	17. misspelled
6. sort before	12. underground	18. misunderstood

Antonyms * Antónimos (page 20)

1. heavy	7. outdoors	13. vanish
2. right	8. straight	14. begin
3. ugly	9. rare	15. fat
4. asleep	10. bright	16. minimum
5. sell	11. full	17. victory
6. absent	12. lose	18. hard

Lesson 4 * Lección 4

Vocabulary * Vocabulario

Things * Cosas

toys
juguetes

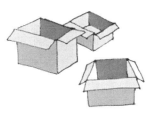

boxes
cajas

string
cuerda

candle
vela

perfume
perfume

gold
oro

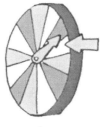

spinner
aguja giratoria

money
dinero

pedal
pedal

ticket
boleto/multa

purse
bolso

balloon
globo

Fill in the Blanks * Llene el Espacio

Llene cada espacio con una palabra de la página de vocabulario.
Use la figura al final de la oración para ayudarse. Lea la oración
con cuidado porque puede necesitar añadir una s o las letras es a la
palabra del vocabulario.

1. Mom will attach a _____string_____ to the kite.

2. He unpacks many _____boxes_____ at work.

3. My mother wears a __gold__ necklace every day.

4. The women buy new ____purses____ on their trip.

5. The red ____balloon____ belongs to the little boy.

6. The girl put the _____money_____ in her pocket.

7. My sister likes to squirt __perfume__ on her wrists.

8. He got five parking __tickets__ in one month.

9. My uncle bought two new __pedals__ for his bike.

10. She will display the new __candle__ in the window.

11. Where is the _____spinner_____ for the game?

12. The boy put all of his __toys__ under the table.

Mountain Biking

Do you like a sport where you can go fast? Do you like to be out in nature? Are you self-reliant? Then you might like mountain biking. This sport requires endurance, bike handling skills and self-reliance. Mountain bikes have knobby tires, large round frame tubing, and suspension or shock absorbers. Most mountain bikers prefer to ride trails called single-track. These are narrow trails that wind through forests or fields.

Many mountain bikers ride at a bike park. Some of these parks are also for snow skiers. In the winter, people take the lifts up and ski down the mountains. In the summer, mountain bikers take the lifts up and ride their bikes down the mountains. There are all levels of rides. If you go down a black diamond trail, you better be prepared for trails that are steep, rocky, narrow, and winding with many hairpin curves. There are other trails that are flatter and wider. These trails are better for beginners or riders who want a slower, less technical ride.

There is special bike equipment for mountain biking. Many riders wear hydration packs. These are backpacks that hold a bladder of water. A long tube is attached to the bladder and runs through a loop in the pack so the end of the tube hangs in front of the rider's shoulder. Riders can drink easily and often using a hydration pack. Other pieces of equipment are a helmet, sunglasses or goggles to keep the dirt and dust out of your eyes, bike gloves, special shoes, and padded shorts. Many people will pack a lightweight jacket and high-energy bars.

Mountain bikers have to be strong, have good endurance and reflexes. Many mountain biking parks do not have chairlifts to carry riders up the mountains. Instead, the riders must pedal up steep grades. Fortunately, mountain bikes have many gears to help the rider pedal up hills. Mountain bikes also have suspension, or shock absorbers, to give the rider a smoother ride over bumpy, rocky trails. The large knobby tires help the rider get good traction on the trail.

After a day of riding, you will be tired and covered in dust and dirt. You may be scratched up from falling off your bike. Maybe, you'll stop someplace for lunch or dinner with your friends. You might talk about the ride and what fun it was to jump over the bumps and race around the curves. You'll probably plan your next ride before you separate to go home to a long hot shower.

Comprehension Questions

Use la información en *Mountain Biking* para contestar las siguientes preguntas. Conteste cada pregunta con una oración completa.

1. Name three things you might see at a mountain bike park.

   _____

2. Name two ways mountain bikes are different from regular bicycles.

   _____

3. What are single-track trails?

   _____

4. Describe a black diamond trail.

   _____

5. What are hydration packs?

   _____

6. Name three pieces of equipment a mountain biker might wear?

   _____

7. Name two things a mountain biker might have in his backpack.

   _____

8. At the end of the ride, what will the rider be covered with?

   _____

9. Would you rather ride a mountain bike or a regular road bicycle? Give three reasons for your answer.

   _____

   _____

   _____

Vocabulary * Vocabulario

Tema – Mountain Biking

Todas las palabras de la tabla siguiente pueden encontrarse en la historia *Mountain Biking*.

Vocabulary Word	Syllable # Clue	Semantic Clue
1. p _ _ _ _	2	a lever that is worked by the foot
2. m _ _ _ _ _ _ _	2	the earth's surface that rises high above sea level
3. g _ _ _ _	1	two or more wheels that have teeth
4. g _ _ _ _ _ _	2	large eyeglases that fit tightly around the eyes to protect them from dust, wind, or glare
5. t _ _ _ _	1	rubber wheels
6. f _ _ _ _ _	2	a thick growth of trees covering a large piece of land
7. t _ _ _ _	1	path
8. f _ _ _ _	1	the support around which a thing is built
9. e _ _ _ _ _ _ _ _	3	the ability to hold up or last under hardship, strain or pain
10. d _ _ _ _ _ _	2	a figure shaped like this: ◇
11. b _ _ _ _ _ _	2	a bag that holds fluids
12. h _ _ _ _ _ _ _ _	3	water
13. h _ _ _ _ _	2	a hard covering to protect the head
14. g _ _ _ _ _	1	covering to protect the hands, with a separate section for each finger and thumb
15. k _ _ _ _ _	2	lumpy

Synonyms * Sinónimos

Escriba, junto a cada palabra, la palabra que signifique lo mismo o casi lo mismo. Use las palabras de la casilla para sus respuestas.

alegar **argue**	1. _____
check	2. _____
Vacilar **hesitate**	3. _____
localizar **locate**	4. _____
object	5. _____
near	6. _____
prance	7. _____
corretear **scamper**	8. _____
inclinado **tilt**	9. _____
often	10. _____
recordar **recall** = *remember*	11. _____
honest	12. _____
liberty	13. _____
easy	14. _____
ayuda **aid**	15. _____
doler **hurt**	16. _____
damejar **squirt**	17. _____
descansa... esto **rest**	18. _____

4	**discover**
10	**frequently**
11	**remember**
1	**disagree**
13	**freedom**
17	**spray**
18	**relax**
16	**harm**
2	**inspect**
8	**run**
15	**assist**
14	**simple**
3	**delay**
7	**leap**
6	**close**
12	**sincere**
9	**slant**
5	**thing**

Answer Key * Las Respuestas

Fill in the Blanks * Llene el Espacio (page 23)

1. string
2. boxes
3. gold
4. purses
5. balloon
6. money
7. perfume
8. tickets
9. pedals
10. candle or candles
11. spinner
12. toys

Comprehension * Comprensión (page 25)

1. At a mountain bike park, you might see lifts, steep trails, or wide trails.
2. Mountain bikes have knobby tires and suspension.
3. Single-track trails are narrow trails.
4. A black diamond trail is steep, rocky, and narrow.
5. Hydration packs hold a bladder of water and have a long tube for drinking.
6. A mountain biker might wear gloves, special shoes, and padded shorts.
7. In his back pack, a mountain biker might have a jacket and energy bars.
8. At the end of the ride, the biker will be covered with dust and dirt.
9. I would like to ride a mountain bike because I like to be out in nature, ride trails, and ride fast.

Vocabulary * Vocabulario (page 26)

1.	pedal	9.	endurance
2.	mountain	10.	diamond
3.	gears	11.	bladder
4.	goggles	12.	hydration
5.	tires	13.	helmet
6.	forest	14.	gloves
7.	trail	15.	knobby
8.	frame		

Synonyms * Sinónimos (page 27)

1.	disagree	7.	leap	13.	freedom
2.	inspect	8.	run	14.	simple
3.	delay	9.	slant	15.	assist
4.	discover	10.	frequently	16.	harm
5.	thing	11.	remember	17.	spray
6.	close	12.	sincere	18.	relax

Lesson 5 * Lección 5

Vocabulary * Vocabulario

Verbs * Verbos

Coloque las palabras de vocabulario en inglés en orden alfabético. Para hacerlo, escriba primero las palabras que comienzan con <u>a</u>, luego las que comienzan con <u>b</u>, después <u>c</u>, <u>d</u>, <u>e</u>, y así sucesivamente. Si dos palabras comienzan con la misma letra, entonces considere la siguiente letra y escriba la palabra que tenga la segunda letra más cercana al principio del alfabeto.

English	Spanish	Alphabetize
1. stir	menear	1. 9
2. plants	plantas	2. 8
3. plays	juega	3. 14
4. helps	ayuda	4. 4
5. wishes	desea	5. 10
6. push	empuja	6. 13
7. winks	guiña	7. 2
8. buzzes	zumba	8. 3
9. asked	preguntó	9. 6
10. locked	cerrar con llave	10. 12
11. spilled	derramó	11. 11
12. rested	descansaron	12. 1
13. painted	pintaron	13. 7
14. called	llamaron	14. 5

Fill in the Blanks * Llene el Espacio

Llene cada espacio con una palabra de la página de vocabulario. Lea la oración con cuidado porque puede necesitar añadir una s o las letras es a la palabra del vocabulario.

1. Many people _____wish_____ to give donations to the charity.

2. Pam _____ at the convention every year.

3. The child _____spills_____ milk on the poster.

4. The girl _asks_ her mom if they could buy the pretty jacket.

5. They _____painted_____ their apartment last weekend.

6. A big bee _____buzzes_____ near a large yellow flower.

7. In the pond, small turtles _____rest_____ on the floating log.

8. _____Plants_____ provide us with beauty and oxygen.

9. The child learns to build when she _____plays_____ with blocks.

10. The dog _____pushes_____ the purple ball around with his nose.

11. The band _____wishes_____ they could perform on the new stage.

12. My father _____winks_____ at my mother from across the table.

13. The boy _____stirs_____ the soup with an enormous spoon.

14. The child accidently _____locked_____ the keys in the car.

Camino de Santiago

Pilgrims have been traveling to Santiago de Compostela in Spain for over fifteen hundred years. Some travel by foot, others by horseback, and still others by bicycle. People make the pilgrimage to visit the shrine where the remains of St. James are buried. Over the years, traffic to the shrine increased bringing with it more roads, bridges, hospices and pilgrimage churches. Towns sprung up along the way to cater to the needs of the traveling pilgrims. The Camino de Santiago is not one route but many extending throughout Europe. All routes lead to Santiago de Compostela in Spain, where the Saint's bones are kept in a crypt beneath the Cathedral's main altar. Guidebooks for this pilgrimage have been around for a long time. The first one was written in the 1300's telling medieval pilgrims where to go, what to wear, how to pray, and alerting them to possible dangers and miracles along the way.

Today, pilgrims each have their own way of making the pilgrimage. Some attend the pilgrim's masses in each town, visiting various churches, monasteries and convents. Others ponder their relationship to their faith and beliefs as they walk the trail. Still others hike for cultural, spiritual, historical, and physical reasons. The symbol of the Santiago pilgrimage is a scallop shell. It often points the way along the routes. The rays of the shell symbolize the different places people come from who go to Santiago. Many pilgrims receive a compostela, certifying them as a pilgrim who has walked the last 100 kilometers of the way to Santiago or has ridden the last 200 kilometers by bicycle.

Would you like to be a pilgrim and travel to the town of Santiago in Spain? If so, how would you go? Would you walk, ride a horse, or pedal a bicycle? Most people choose to walk. They carry their clothes and sleeping bags on their backs. They walk many miles a day. Sometimes getting up at four o'clock in the morning to start their day's journey. This way they can walk in the cool morning hours before it gets hot. Other's get up early so they can walk twenty to thirty miles in a day. At night the pilgrims stay in refuges where they have a bed in a room full of bunk beds. They put their sleeping bag down on the bunk for a much needed rest. The pilgrims buy their food in the small towns to make a picnic along the way.

Other pilgrims travel with a tour group. They may walk only eight to twelve miles a day. They sleep in more comfortable lodgings. They do not need to carry a sleeping bag. This way, of course, is more expensive. Whichever way a person decides to travel the Camino de Santiago, they will have time to think and experience the magnificent countryside and small villages along the way.

Comprehension Questions

Use la información en *Camino de Santiago* para contestar las siguientes preguntas. Conteste cada pregunta con una oración completa.

1. How long have pilgrims been traveling to Santiago de Compostela?

   Pilgrims have been traveling ...

2. What do the pilgrims visit at Santiago de Compostela?

   The pilgrims visit the sanctuary at S de C.

3. When was the first guidebook written for the Camino de Santiago?

   The first guidebook was written in thirteen hundreds.

4. What is the symbol of the Santiago pilgrimage?

   The symbol of S de C is the scallop shell.

5. Why do some people receive a Compostela certificate?

   Some people receive a Compostela certificate because they walked or rode many miles.

6. In what country is Santiago de Compostela?

   Santiago de Compostela is in Spain.
   se quedan - permanecer.

7. Where do many people stay at night if they want inexpensive lodging?

   Many people stay at night in refuges.

8. What are two reasons people get up early to start walking the Camino?

   _____

9. If you were a pilgrim, how would you want to travel the Camino de Santiago?

   _____

   _____

   _____

Suffixes * Sufijos

El sufijo ed indica una acción en el pasado. Existen tres sonidos para el sufijo ed: /ed/ como en *planted*, /d/ como en *called*, y /t/ como en *helped*. Cuando añada un sufijo a una palabra que termina en una e muda, elimine la e si el sufijo comienza con una vocal. No elimine la e si el sufijo comienza con una consonante.

Añada ed a cada una de las siguientes palabras de acción (verbos). Luego escriba qué sonido tiene la terminación ed. La primera ya está hecha.

Verb	Add the suffix ed	Sound ed makes: /t/, /ed/, /d/
1. jump	*jumped*	/t/
2. splash	splashed	/d/
3. like	liked	(t)
4. float	floated flotar	(ed)
5. laugh	laughed	(d)
6. live	lived	(d)
7. shout	shouted gritar	(ed)
8. climb	climbed	(d)

Complete cada oración con una de las palabras anteriores que tenga el sufijo ed.

9. At the apartment's pool, the teenagers _____splashed_____ in the water.

10. On the field, the coach ___shouted___ the instructions to the team.

11. The kids ___jumped___ when their friend squirted them with water.

12. George Washington _____lived_____ a long time ago.

13. When they were young, the boys _liked_ to play with electric trains.

14. The boy ___jumped___ in the puddle and got his shoes and pants wet.

15. The cat quickly _climbed_ the tree when the dog came into the yard.

16. The girls ___floated___ down the river on their homemade raft.

33

Antonyms, Synonyms, or Homophones
Antónimos, Sinónimos, o Homófonos

Lea cada par de palabras. Luego decida si cada par es un *antónimo*, *sinónimo*, u *homófono*. La primera ya está hecha.

Pair of Words	Antonym	Synonym	Homophone
1. knot & not			X
2. rocky & smooth	✓		
3. herd & heard			✓
4. inside & outside	✗		
5. dirt & soil		✓	
6. asked & answered	✓		
7. decay & rot		✓	
8. chili & chilly			✓
9. begin & start		✓	
10. softly & loudly	✓		
11. helps & assists		✓	
12. throw & toss		✓	
13. sleepy & awake	✓		
14. swift & fast		✓	
15. pull & push	✓		
16. bare & bear			✓
17. bush & shrub		✓	
18. burrow & burro			✓
19. talk & chat		✓	
20. drizzle & sprinkle		✓	
21. complete & finish		✓	
22. kind & mean	✓		

Answer Key * Las Respuestas

Alphabetizing * Colocar en orden alfabético (page 29)

1. asked	5. locked	9. push	13. winks
2. buzzes	6. painted	10. rested	14. wishes
3. called	7. plants	11. spilled	
4. helps	8. plays	12. stir	

Fill in the Blanks * Llene el Espacio (page 30)

1. called
2. helps
3. spilled
4. asked
5. painted
6. buzzes
7. rested
8. Plants
9. plays
10. pushed
11. wishes
12. winks
13. stirs
14. locked

Comprehension * Comprensión (page 32)

1. Pilgrims have been traveling to Santiago de Compostela for over fifteen hundred years.
2. The pilgrims visit the shrine where the remains of St. James are buried.
3. The first guidebook was written in the 1300's.
4. The symbol of the pilgrimage is a scallop shell.
5. A certificate is given to the pilgrims who walk the last 100 kilometers or ride a bicycle the last 200 kilometers to Santiago.
6. Santiago de Compostela is located in Spain.
7. For inexpensive lodging, people stay in refuges.
8. People start walking early to avoid the heat and to walk many miles.
9. I would travel with a tour group and stay in comfortable lodgings.

Suffixes * Sufijos (page 33)

1. jumped	/t/	7. shouted	/ed/	13. liked	
2. splashed	/t/	8. climbed	/d/	14. jumped	
3. liked	/t/	9. splashed		15. climbed	
4. floated	/ed/	10. shouted		16. floated	
5. laughed	/t/	11. laughed			
6. lived	/d/	12. lived			

Antyonyms, Synonyms or Homophones * Antónimos, Sinónimos, o Homófonos (page 34)

1. homophone	9. synonym	17. synonym
2. antonym	10. antonym	18. homophone
3. homophone	11. synonym	19. synonym
4. antonym	12. synonym	20. synonym
5. synonym	13. antonym	21. synonym
6. antonym	14. synonym	22. antonym
7. synonym	15. antonym	
8. homophone	16. homophone	

Lesson 6 * Lección 6

Vocabulary * Vocabulario

Food * Alimentos

produce
productos agrícolas

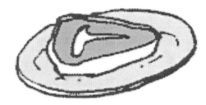

steak
bistec

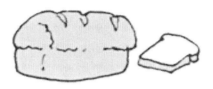

bread
pan

sugar
azúcar

oatmeal
harina de avena

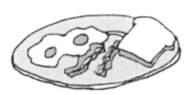

breakfast
desayuno

coffee
café

brisket
carne de pecho

salt
sal

pepper
pimienta

watermelon
sandía

broccoli
brócoli

Fill in the Blanks * Llene el Espacio

Llene cada espacio con una palabra de la página de vocabulario. Use la figura al final de la oración para ayudarse. Lea la oración con cuidado porque puede necesitar añadir una <u>s</u> o las letras <u>es</u> a la palabra del vocabulario.

1. When Tom was in the army he drank _coffee_ .

2. Dad fixes a big _breakfast_ every morning.

3. I will put the _bread_ in the toaster.

4. The boy passes the _broccoli_ to his mother.

5. Dad will cook the _brisket_ in the crockpot.

6. Do not put too much _sugar_ on your cereal.

7. The _pepper_ shaker is in the kitchen cupboard.

8. This store always has fresh _produce_ .

9. My mom likes her _steak_ well done.

10. At the picnic, they had a _watermelon_ seed spitting contest.

11. Every morning for breakfast, Tom has a bowl of _oatmeal_ .

12. Eating too much _salt_ is not good for your health.

Brine Shrimp

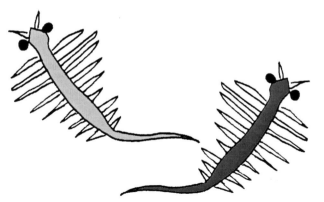

Would you like a pet that does not cost much money to buy or keep? Would you like a pet that does not take much care? You will not need to walk this pet. You will not need to brush this pet. You will not have expensive vet bills. You may not even need to feed this pet. No, it is not a pet rock! It is brine shrimp.

Brine shrimp are a type of aquatic crustacean. Crustaceans are animals that have a hard outer shell and usually live in water. Brine shrimp are found worldwide in saltwater, though not in oceans. Brine shrimp eggs can stay un-hatched for several years in dry conditions, even at temperatures below freezing. But once placed in water, the eggs hatch within a few hours, and will grow to be about one centimeter long. Brine shrimp have a life span of about one year.

Another name for brine shrimp are sea monkeys. You can buy a sea monkey kit. The kit will contain several small packages. You will need a bowl of water. On day one, you add the package with eggs and salt to the water. On day two, you add the package that contains more eggs, Epson salts, borax, soda, yeast, and a blue dye. The blue dye is used to make the hatched animals more visible. You will see sea monkeys by the second day. You may need a magnifying glass because they are so small! The nauplii, or larvae, are less than 500 micrometers when they first hatch and will grow to be one centimeter long. Brine shrimp eat micro-algae, yeast, wheat flour, soybean powder or egg yolk. In your kit, there will also be a food package and a boost package to keep your shrimp healthy and active. Even though a sea monkey's life span is one year, the kit may say the sea-monkeys will live up to two years. This is because the colony may be able to sustain itself for two years.

Another way you can have a brine shrimp pet is by purchasing a biosphere. This is more expensive than a sea monkey kit. A biosphere is a totally enclosed ecosystem in a glass sphere. Inside the biosphere are brine shrimp, algae, wood, water and air. Many biospheres are a work of art. They have been carefully crafted to provide peace and beauty.

Do you think you would like brine shrimp as a pet? They won't take much work. If you have a biosphere, all you will need to do is give it indirect light and a mild temperature. You won't even need to feed it. With brine shrimp, when you go on vacation, you will not need to worry about who will take care of your pet.

Comprehension Questions

Use la información en *Brine Shrimp* para contestar las siguientes preguntas. Conteste cada pregunta con una oración completa.

1. What are brine shrimp?

   _____

2. What do brine shrimp eggs need to hatch?

   _____

3. How big are brine shrimp?

   _____

4. What is another name for brine shrimp?

   _____

5. What two words are homophones in this story?

   _all ala_____

6. What is a synonym for purchase?   _comprar._

   _____buy_____

7. What is a crustacean?

   _____

8. What shape is a sphere? Give an example of something that is a sphere.

   _____

9. Would you like brine shrimp for a pet? Give two reasons for your answer.

   _____

   _____

   _____

Suffixes * Sufijos

Un sufijo es un grupo de letras que se añaden al final de una palabra para cambiar su significado. En esta página usaremos los siguientes sufijos: -ful, -less, -ous. Los sufijos -ful y -ous significan *llenos de*. El sufijo -less significa *sin*.

Escriba el significado de cada una de las siguientes palabras. La primera ya está hecha.

1. **harmless**
   without harm

2. **successful**
   _____

3. **weightless**
   _____

4. **joyous**
   _____

5. **graceful**
   _____

6. **cheerful**
   _____

7. **wonderful**
   _____

8. **powerless**
   _____

9. **dangerous**
   _____

10. **careless**
   _____

Complete cada oración con una de las palabras anteriores.

11. It is ___dangerous___ to ride your bike at night.

12. My grandmother had a smile on her face and was very ___joyous___ .

13. He felt ___powerless___ as his car skidded on the ice.

14. The children had a ___wonderful___ time at the amusement park.

15. The feather is almost ___weightless___ .

16. The boy was messy and ___careless___ with his homework.

17. The ___graceful___ dancers leaped across the stage.

18. My mother is a ___successful___ business woman.

40

Idioms * Modismos

Un modismo es una expresión o frase cuyo significado puede no estar relacionado al significado de las palabras en la expresión o frase. Por ejemplo: "keep your eyes peeled (pela los ojos)" significa *mira con cuidado*.

Idiom	Meaning
raining cats and dogs	raining very hard
Cat got your tongue?	Is there a reason you're not speaking?
fly off the handle	to lose your temper quickly
one-track mind	always thinking about just one thing
once in a blue moon	very seldom, almost never
nutty as a fruitcake	crazy or extremely strange
I'm all ears.	I'm eager to listen
hit the nail on the head	to be exactly correct
by the skin of your teeth	a really close call, just barely
throw in the towel	to give up, or to quit
keep your eyes peeled	look carefully

Complete cada oración con uno de los modismos anteriores.

1. This morning, we made it to school *by the skin of our teeth*

2. My brother often *hits the nail on the head* with his answers.

3. My sister has a *one-track mind* when it comes to what she wants to do.

4. My aunt, with her purple and red hair, is as *nutty as a fruitcake* .

5. When the boy did not say anything, the coach said, "*I'm all ears* ?"

6. My father said, *keep your eyes peeled* , when we were looking for a place to eat.

7. Please do not *lose your temper quickly* when you're at work.

8. We will not *throw in the towel* during this competition.

9. We took our umbrellas because it was *raining very hard* .

10. We see our uncle *very seldom / almost never* .

11. My brother was _____ when my dad told him about the new motorcycle.

41

Answer Key * Las Respuestas

Fill in the Blanks * Llene el Espacio (page 37)

1. coffee
2. breakfast
3. bread
4. broccoli
5. brisket
6. sugar
7. pepper
8. produce
9. steak
10. watermelon
11. oatmeal
12. salt

Comprehension * Comprensión (page 39)

1. Brine shrimp are a type of aquatic crustacean.
2. To hatch, the eggs need to be placed in water.
3. Brine shrimp grow to be one centimeter long.
4. Another name for brine shrimp are sea monkeys.
5. See and sea are homophones.
6. A synonym for purchase is buy.
7. A crustacean is an animal that has a hard outer shell and usually lives in water.
8. A sphere is round. A ball is a sphere.
9. I would like brine shrimp for a pet because they are inexpensive to keep and do not require much care.

Suffixes * Sufijos (page 40)

1. without harm	7. filled with wonder	13. powerless
2. filled with success	8. without power	14. wonderful
3. without weight	9. filled with danger	15. weightless
4. filled with joy	10. without care	16. careless
5. filled with grace	11. dangerous	17. graceful
6. filled with cheer	12. cheerful	18. successful

Idioms * Modismos (page 41)

1. by the skin of our teeth
2. hits the nail on the head
3. one-track mind
4. nutty as a fruitcake
5. Cat got your tongue?
6. keep your eyes peeled
7. fly off the handle
8. throw in the towel
9. raining cats and dogs
10. once in a blue moon
11. all ears

Lesson 7 * Lección 7

Vocabulary * Vocabulario

Clothes * Ropa

shirt
camisa

skirt
falda

closet
armario

ruffle
volante

iron
plancha

shoe
zapato

fur
piel

sweater
suéter

jacket
chaqueta

pocket
bolsillo

sew
coser

stripe
raya

Fill in the Blanks * Llene el Espacio

Llene cada espacio con una palabra de la página de vocabulario. Use la figura al final de la oración para ayudarse. Lea la oración con cuidado porque puede necesitar añadir una <u>s</u> o las letras <u>es</u> o <u>ed</u> a la palabra del vocabulario.

1. **Dad picked up five** _shirts_ **at the dry cleaners.**

2. **The girls** _sewed_ **fancy costumes for the party.**

3. **Sam is wearing a shirt with blue and red** _stripes_ .

4. **This evening, my sister plans to hem her new** _skirt_ .

5. **That brown** _sweater_ **belongs to my brother.**

6. **I need to fix the hole in my** _pocket_ .

7. **You have too many clothes in your** _closet_ .

8. **The boy got dirt on his new** _shoe_ .

9. **My sister bought a blouse with pink** _ruffles_ .

10. **Dad** _irons_ **the girls' dresses for the birthday party.**

11. **Pam bought a winter coat that has** _fur_ **on the collar and cuffs.**

12. **Kim's** _jacket_ **has the company's logo on the back.**

Fashion Models

Have you ever been to a fashion show? Sometimes department stores will have fashion shows. They will set up a runway, chairs, and serve refreshments in hopes that afterwards you will shop in the different sections of the store.

There are different types of models. When people hear the word fashion model, they often think of the high fashion models. These models work for high fashion designers and are featured in fashion magazines. Clothing designers usually have an annual fashion show. Models will walk the "catwalk" displaying the new clothes. High fashion models are generally from 5 foot 9 inches to 6 feet tall and very thin. A 5 foot 9 inch model will weigh from 105-107 pounds and wear a size 0-4. Typically a high fashion model will have 32-35" bust, 22-25" waist, and 33-36" hips. These models have strong, unique, and distinctive features.

Another type of modeling is commercial modeling. These models work for catalogues, cosmetic companies, and swimsuit designers. Catalogue models can vary in their weight and height depending on the clothes they are modeling. Plus-size clothes need plus-size models. Cosmetic models work for makeup companies. Most cosmetic models have the high fashion body type. These models work for television commercials, magazine advertisements, and billboards. Swimsuit models are usually fitness models displaying an athletic and healthy physique with beautiful female curves.

Hip hop models are female models who appear in hip hop videos, magazines, and calendars. They are also known as hip hop honeys, dimes, video vixens and eye candy.

We see fashion models everyday. We see them in magazines, on TV, and on billboards. Fashion models are men and women. Where was the last fashion model you saw?

Comprehension Questions

Use la información en *Fashion Models* para contestar las siguientes preguntas. Conteste cada pregunta con una oración completa.

1. Name one reason why department stores have fashion shows.

   _____

2. Name five types of models.

   _____

3. Which type of model is most often on the cover of fashion magazines.

   _____

4. What's the "catwalk"?

   _____

5. Describe a high fashion model.

   _____

6. Where do commercial models work?

   _____

7. Why must catalogue models be all sizes?

   _____

8. Name three places where you will see models.

   _____

9. What are hip hop models?

   _____

10. Could you be a model? Why or Why not?

   _____

Analogies * Analogías

Las analogías son comparaciones. Muestran relaciones entre palabras. Complete cada analogía a continuación. Use las palabras a la derecha para sus respuestas. La primera ya está hecha.

1. Acorn is to squirrel as _____*honey*_____ is to bear.

2. Shirt is to boy as _____ is to girl.

3. Toys are to children as _____ are to men.

4. _____ is to bee as peep is to chick.

5. _____ is to vacation as work is to job.

6. Dad is to father as mom is to _____ .

7. Woman is to women as man is to _____ .

8. Shrimp is to saltwater as frog is to _____ .

9. Four sides is to _____ as three sides is to triangle.

10. Shoe is to foot as _____ is to head.

11. Car is to _____ as boat is to river.

12. Grandpa is to grandma as _____ is to aunt.

13. Bear is to forest as monkey is to _____ .

14. Small is to cabin as _____ is to mansion

15. Carrots is to produce as beef is to _____ .

16. Food is to chewing as soda is to _____ .

17. _____ is to hospital as teacher is to school.

huge
nurse
uncle
tools
street
honey
buzz
freshwater
drinking
blouse
jungle
relax
hat
meat
square
mother
men

Suffixes * Sufijos

Un sufijo es un grupo de letras que se añaden al final de una palabra para cambiar su significado. En esta página usaremos los siguientes sufijos: -ly, -en, -est, -ness. El sufijo -ly significa *cómo* o *hasta qué grado*; -en significa *hacer o hecho de*; -est significa *lo más*; -ness significa *que tiene*. Use las palabras a la derecha para sus respuestas.

1. Dad will _____ the kitchen knives.

2. The old woman likes to do random acts of _____ .

3. His aunt is recovering from a long _____ .

4. Pam's dog brings her much _____ .

5. My sister does _____ in school.

6. A snail is one of the _____ creatures.

7. We will _____ help our mother after school.

8. You need a flashlight to walk in _____ .

9. The boy with all the muscles is the _____ .

10. The Pilgrims ate with _____ dishes.

11. Her son gets _____ progress reports at school.

12. My brother plans to _____ his hair on Saturday.

13. The _____ box will not fit in the closet.

14. He can not see because of his _____ .

15. My father always speaks very _____ .

16. I will pack my _____ sweater for the trip.

17. My sister is the _____ runner on the track team.

48

| weekly |
| poorly |
| softly |
| gladly |
| sharpen |
| wooden |
| woolen |
| straighten |
| slowest |
| biggest |
| strongest |
| fastest |
| illness |
| darkness |
| happiness |
| blindness |
| kindness |

Answer Key * Las Respuestas

Fill in the Blanks * Llene el Espacio (page 44)

1. shirts
2. sew
3. stripes
4. skirt
5. sweater
6. pocket
7. closet
8. shoes
9. ruffles
10. ironed
11. fur
12. jacket

Comprehension * Comprensión (page 46)

1. The department stores hope that people attending the fashion show will later shop in the store.
2. High fashion, commercial, catalogue, cosmetic, and swimsuit are different types of models.
3. High fashion models are most often on the cover of magazines.
4. The "cat walk" is the runway where the models walk to display their clothes.
5. A high fashion model is tall and thin, with distinctive features.
6. Commercial models work for catalogues, cosmetic companies, and swimsuit designers.
7. Catalogue models must be different sizes because they model different types of clothing.
8. You will see models on TV, in magazines, and on billboards.
9. Hip hop models are female models who appear in hip hop videos, magazines, and calendars.
10. I could be a catalogue model because a catalogue model doesn't have to be tall and slim, but can be any height or weight.

Analogies * Analogías (page 47)

1. honey	7. men	13. jungle
2. blouse	8. freshwater	14. huge
3. tools	9. square	15. meat
4. buzz	10. hat	16. drinking
5. relax	11. street	17. nurse
6. mother	12. uncle	

Suffixes * Sufijos (page 48)

1. sharpen	7. gladly	13. biggest
2. kindness	8. darkness	14. blindness
3. illness	9. strongest	15. softly
4. happiness	10. wooden	16. woolen
5. poorly	11. weekly	17. fastest
6. slowest	12. straighten	

Lesson 8 * Lección 8

Vocabulary * Vocabulario

Home * Casa

table
mesa

kitchen
cocina

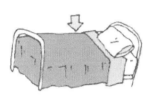

blanket
manta

door
puerta

floor
piso

apartment
apartamento

screen
pantalla

fireplace
chimenea

piano
piano

mirror
espejo

computer
computadora

radio
radio

Fill in the Blanks * Llene el Espacio

Llene cada espacio con una palabra de la página de vocabulario.
Use la figura al final de la oración para ayudarse. Lea la oración
con cuidado porque puede necesitar añadir una s o las letras es a la
palabra del vocabulario.

1. The children live in an _____ .

2. All the doors and windows have _____ .

3. Many people listen to the _____ for news
    and entertainment.

4. We will clean the _____ on Saturday.

5. They will hang a large _____ in their livingroom.

6. She likes to sit in front of the _____ and read.

7. Please put your donations in the box on the _____ .

8. _____ are very useful to many people.

9. Pam will put a wreath on the front _____ .

10. He has taken _____ lessons for ten years.

11. Please deliver the packages to the first _____ .

12. My sister uses an electric _____ in the winter.

Mosquitoes

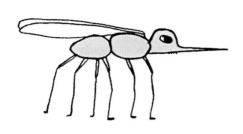

Slap! Scratch! Spray! How many times have you been bitten by mosquitoes? If you're male, overweight, and have type O blood, you may have a better chance of being bitten. Mosquitoes are extremely sensitive to the carbon dioxide exhaled by mammals and to several substances found in sweat. Mosquitoes can detect heat, so they find warm-blooded mammals easily. Female mosquitoes are the blood-suckers; whereas, male mosquitoes do not have the mouth parts suitable for sucking blood. When the female bites, she also injects an anticoagulant (anti-clotting chemical) to keep the victim's blood flowing.

Mosquitoes have been around for over 30 million years. Like all insects, mosquitoes have three body parts (head, thorax, and abdomen), a hard exoskeleton, and six legs. Mosquitoes also have a pair of wings. They have a straw-like proboscis and can only eat liquids. Mosquitoes undergo a complete metamorphosis. They go through four distinct stages of development. The four stages are egg, larva, pupa, and adult. The full life cycle of a mosquito takes about a month. Females lay from 40 to 400 tiny white eggs in standing or very slow-moving water. Within a week, the eggs hatch into larva. Larvae eat bits of floating organic matter. Next is the pupa stage. During this stage, they live just below the water's surface and do not eat. After a few days the adult emerges from the pupa. The adult lives only a few weeks.

In many parts of the world, mosquitoes are a major health problem. They can transmit diseases. In other countries, mosquito bites are mostly just a nuisance. One type of mosquito carries malaria, and most species of mosquito can carry the West Nile virus. The West Nile virus came to the United States in 1999; and by 2003, had spread to almost every state. Most people infected with the WNV will not show any symptoms. However, a few can suffer from a high fever, headache, neck stiffness, vision loss, and other symptoms that can last several weeks.

Homeowners can eliminate mosquito breeding grounds by removing stagnant water. Look for sitting water in your yard. Are there old tires, cans, buckets, or tree stumps containing water? Mosquitoes do not need much water to lay their eggs. Removing mosquito-breeding areas can be extremely effective in reducing the mosquito population.

Most mosquitoes are nocturnal. So when you go out at night, wear long pants and long sleeves to protect your skin. Use an insect repellant containing DEET. If you are bitten, soak in a warm oatmeal bath for 10-15 minutes. If you don't have time for that you can apply calamine lotion, white toothpaste, or a liquid antacid to your bites.

Comprehension Questions

Use la información en *Mosquitoes* para contestar las siguientes preguntas. Conteste cada pregunta con una oración completa.

1. Do male or female mosquitoes bite humans?

   _____

2. How long have mosquitoes been on Earth?

   _____

3. What is complete metamorphosis?

   _____

4. Where do mosquitoes lay their eggs?

   _____

5. How long is the life cycle of most mosquitoes?

   _____

6. Why are mosquitoes a major health problem in some countries?

   _____

7. What are some symptoms of the West Nile virus?

   _____

8. What can you do at home to get rid of mosquitoes?

   _____

9. What can you do to prevent mosquito bites?

   _____

10. Name two types of first aid for mosquito bites.

   _____

Similes * Símiles

Un símil es una forma de hablar que enlaza dos cosas que no se parecen usando las palabras *like* o *as*.

Use las palabras a la derecha para completar los siguientes símiles comunes. La primera ya está hecha.

1. As happy as a ___*lark*___ .		board
2. As blind as a _____ .		lark
3. As light as a _____ .		nails
4. As busy as a _____ .		cucumber
5. As cool as a _____ .		owl
6. As good as _____ .		snow
7. As white as _____ .		bee
8. As flat as a _____ .		daisy
9. As hard as _____ .		picture
10. As black as _____ .		feather
11. As pretty as a _____ .		mule
12. As cute as a _____ .		ice
13. As wise as an _____ .		pancake
14. As stubborn as an _____ .		bat
15. As cold as _____ .		gold
16. As stiff as a _____ .		coal
17. As fresh as a _____ .		button

54

Catagories * Categorías

Lea las palabras a la derecha y después escríbalas bajo la categoría correcta.

Birds

1. _____
2. _____
3. _____

Flowers

4. _____
5. _____
6. _____

Mammals

7. _____
8. _____
9. _____

Minerals

10. _____
11. _____
12. _____

Food

13. _____
14. _____
15. _____

Insects

16. _____
17. _____
18. _____

Tools

19. _____
20. _____
21. _____

Weather

22. _____
23. _____
24. _____

rain
lark
nails
cucumber
owl
snow
bee
daisy
ox
hammer
mule
rose
pancake
bat
gold
coal
drill
silver
bread
butterfly
tulip
beetle
robin
sleet

55

Answer Key * Las Respuestas

Fill in the Blanks * Llene el Espacio (page 51)

1. apartment
2. screens
3. radio
4. kitchen
5. mirror
6. fireplace
7. table
8. computers
9. door
10. piano
11. floor
12. blanket

Comprehension * Comprensión (page 53)

1. Female mosquitoes bite humans.
2. Mosquitoes have been on earth for over 30 million years.
3. Four distinct stages of development complete the metamorphosis of the mosquito.
4. Mosquitoes lay their eggs in standing or slow moving water.
5. The life cycle of a mosquito is about a month.
6. Mosquitoes can transmit diseases.
7. Some people have no symptoms. Others have a fever, headache, and neck stiffness.
8. At home, removing stagnant water will help get rid of mosquitoes.
9. Wearing long sleeves, long pants, and repellant with DEET will help prevent bites.
10. Two types of first aid for bites are soaking in a warm oatmeal bath and applying calamine lotion.

Similes * Símiles (page 54)

1. lark	7. snow	13. owl
2. bat	8. pancake	14. mule
3. feather	9. nails	15. ice
4. bee	10. coal	16. board
5. cucumber	11. picture	17. daisy
6. gold	12. button	

Catagories * Categorías (page 55)

1. lark	9. bat	17. butterfly
2. owl	10. gold	18. beetle
3. robin	11. coal	19. nails
4. daisy	12. silver	20. hammer
5. rose	13. cucumber	21. drill
6. tulip	14. pancake	22. rain
7. ox	15. bread	23. snow
8. mule	16. bee	24. sleet

Lesson 9 * Lección 9

Vocabulary * Vocabulario

Nature * Naturaleza

rain
lluvia

flower
flor

dawn
amanecer

soil
suelo

night
noche

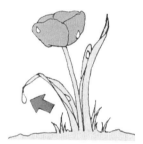

dew
rocío

cloud
nube

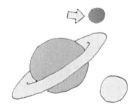

planet
planeta

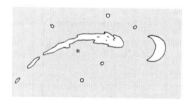

comet
cometa

pumpkin
calabaza

tadpole
renacuajo

tornado
tornado

Fill in the Blanks * Llene el Espacio

Llene cada espacio con una palabra de la página de vocabulario. Use la figura al final de la oración para ayudarse. Lea la oración con cuidado porque puede necesitar añadir una <u>s</u> o las letras <u>es</u> a la palabra del vocabulario.

1. Today there are many _____ in the sky.

2. We can look at the _____ through a telescope.

3. The _____ is moist in the shade under the tree.

4. The boy will carve a face on the _____ .

5. The_____ will turn into frogs.

6. In the morning, the grass is wet from the _____ .

7. She has many beautiful _____ in her garden.

8. When there is a _____ warning, they go down into their basement.

9. At _____ the sky is full of stars.

10. Last night we saw a _____ with a long tail.

11. Meg likes to walk in the _____ with an umbrella.

12. My dad and his friends go fishing at _____ .

Mount Everest

Mount Everest is the highest point on Earth. It is 8,848 meters or 29,028 feet above sea level. It is part of the Himalaya range in Asia and is located on the border between Nepal and China. If you want to climb Mt. Everest, you will need to go through the Death Zone.

In the Death Zone, at 8,000 meters and higher, your body functions begin to deteriorate. You can lose consciousness and die all because of lack of oxygen. At the summit of Mt. Everest there is only a third of the oxygen that is available at sea level. Temperatures can dip to very low levels, resulting in frostbite of any body part exposed to the air. High winds on Everest can also make it very difficult for climbers. Most climbers spend less than thirty minutes on "top of the world" because they need to descend before afternoon weather becomes a serious problem or darkness sets in.

In 1953 Edmund Hillary and Tenzing Norgay were the first climbers ever to reach the top of Mount Everest. Before ascending to the peak on May 28, 1953, they made camp at 8,503 meters spending a cold night trying to sleep. Above 7,500 meters sleeping becomes very difficult, and digesting food is impossible as the body shuts the digestive system down. At 4'oclock in the morning, they rose and prepared for their ascent. Using oxygen equipment, they departed for the summit at 6:30 in the morning and reached the summit at 11:30 a.m. At the summit, they paused to take photographs and buried a few pieces of candy and a small cross in the snow before descending. Hillary took a photo of Tenzing Norgay at the summit waving his ice ax which flew the flags of Great Britain, Nepal, the United Nations and India. Edmund Hillary was from New Zealand and Tenzing Norgay was a Sherpa from Nepal. It was a team effort for them to reach the summit. John Hunt led the British expedition and many Sherpas carried equipment to the base camps. Afterwards, Queen Elizabeth II knighted both Hunt and Hillary for their efforts.

If you would like to climb Mr. Everest, you will need a lot of money. The often-quoted fee for a guided climb is $65,000, though the price varies depending on the size of the expedition and the outfitter. In addition, you will need equipment that will probably run at least $8,000 just for the basics. If you want to take a satellite phone, digital camera, laptop and other luxury items, the cost will probably go to at least $16,000. Don't forget, you'll need to be in excellent physical condition. Most expedition operators require a climbing resume, which often needs to include an 8,000 meter climb. So before you buy your ticket to Katmandu, Nepal, you will need to do some research and a lot of exercise.

Comprehension Questions

Use la información en *Mount Everest* para contestar las siguientes preguntas. Conteste cada pregunta con una oración completa.

1. Where is Mount Everest?

   _____

2. Why do you need oxygen in the Death Zone?

   _____

3. Who were the first climbers to reach the summit of Mount Everest?

   _____

4. When did these first climbers reach the summit of Mt. Everest?

   _____

5. Who carried equipment to the base camps for these two climbers?

   _____

6. Who was John Hunt?

   _____

7. What are three things you would need to climb Mount Everest?

   _____

8. What is the capital of Nepal?

   _____

9. Would you like to climb Mount Everest? Give two reasons for your answer.

   _____

   _____

   _____

Analogies * Analogías

Las analogías son comparaciones. Muestran relaciones entre palabras. Complete cada analogía a continuación. Use las palabras a la derechas para sus respuestas. La primera ya está hecha.

1. Feather is to bird as _____ is to mammal.

2. Pork is to pig as _____ is to cow.

3. Grandfather is to _____ as baby is to young.

4. Black is to coal as yellow is to _____ .

5. Hat is to _____ as glove is to hand.

6. Less is to subtraction as _____ is to addition.

7. _____ is to funny as cry is to sad.

8. Sixty seconds is to minute as 60 minutes is to _____ .

9. Slow is to turtle as _____ is to rabbit.

10. Enormous is to huge as tiny is to _____ .

11. Legs are to _____ as wings are to fly.

12. Butter is to _____ as sugar is to coffee.

13. Ball is to soccer as puck is to _____ .

14. _____ is to cold as fever is to flu.

15. _____ is to foot as wrist is to hand.

16. _____ is to water as hunger is to food.

17. Wool is to _____ as cotton is to shirt.

thirst
walk
laugh
old
small
fur
sweater
hockey
ankle
more
steak
cough
head
hour
gold
fast
bread

Vocabulary * Vocabulario

Todas las palabras de la tabla siguiente pueden encontrarse en la historia *Mount Everest.*

Vocabulary Word	Syllable # Clue	Semantic Clue
1. d _ _ _ _ _ _	2	to move down to a lower place
2. o _ _ _ _ _ _ _ _	3	a business that sells equipment, clothes and services
3. r _ _ _ _ _ _	3	a short account of a person's career and qualifications
4. e _ _ _ _ _ _ _ _	4	a long journey by a group of people to explore a region
5. p _ _ _	1	the pointed top of a mountain
6. d_ _ _ _ _ _ _ _	5	become progressively worse
7. f _ _	1	a payment that is asked or given for services
8. r _ _ _ _	1	a row or line of connected mountains
9. k _ _ _ _ _ _ _	2	to give the rank of knight to
10. f _ _ _ _ _ _ _ _	2	damage to the ears, toes, or other parts of the body caused by exposure to very cold temperatures
11. s _ _ _ _ _	2	the top of a mountain
12. a _ _ _ _ _	2	climbing up
13. l _ _ _ _ _	3	something that is not really needed but gives comfort and pleasure
14. s _ _ _ _ _ _ _ _	3	a man-made object that has been put into orbit around the earth
15. o _ _ _ _ _	3	a gas that is needed by living things

62

Answer Key * Las Respuestas

Fill in the Blanks * Llene el Espacio (page 58)

1. clouds
2. planets or planet
3. soil
4. pumpkin
5. tadpoles
6. dew
7. flowers
8. tornado
9. night
10. comet
11. rain
12. dawn

Comprehension * Comprensión (page 60)

1. Mount Everest is located on the border between Nepal and China.
2. There is not enough oxygen in the Death Zone to sustain body functions.
3. The first climbers to reach the summit were Edmund Hillary and Tenzing Norgay.
4. They reached the summit at 11:30 am on May 28, 1953.
5. Sharpas carried the equipment to the base camp.
6. John Hunt led the British expedition.
7. You would need a guide, equipment, and be in good physical condition.
8. Katmandu is the capital of Nepal.
9. I would not like to climb Mount Everest because it is a very difficult climb and the weather is harsh.

Analogies * Analogías (page 61)

1. fur	7. Laugh	13. hockey
2. steak	8. hour	14. Cough
3. old	9. fast	15. Ankle
4. gold	10. small	16. Thirst
5. head	11. walk	17. sweater
6. more	12. bread	

Vocabulary * Vocabulario (page 62)

1. descend	6. deteriorate	11. summit
2. outfitter	7. fee	12. ascend
3. resume	8. range	13. luxury
4. expedition	9. knighted	14. satellite
5. peak	10. frostbite	15. oxygen

Lesson 10 * Lección 10

Vocabulary * Vocabulario

The Body * El cuerpo

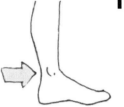

ankle
tobillo

stomach
estómago

head
cabeza

heart
corazón

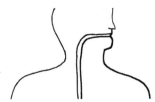

throat
garganta

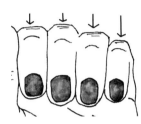

knuckles
nudillos

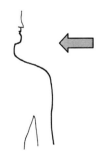

shoulder
hombro

fingernails
uñas de las manos

toenails
uñas de los pies

old
viejo

curl
rizar

perspire
transpirar

Fill in the Blanks * Llene el Espacio

Llene cada espacio con una palabra de la página de vocabulario. Use la figura al final de la oración para ayudarse. Lea la oración con cuidado porque puede necesitar añadir una <u>s</u> o las letras <u>es</u> a la palabra del vocabulario.

1. **He has a tattoo on his left** _____ .

2. **Your** _____ **is about the size of your fist.**

3. **She wears a bracelet on her** _____ .

4. **She polishes her** _____ **once a month.**

5. **That boy is always cracking his** _____ .

6. **My dad** _____ **a lot when he works in the yard.**

7. **Tom is in bed with a sore** _____ .

8. **Pam broke her** _____ **when she fell off her bike.**

9. **Meg** _____ **her hair with rollers twice a week.**

10. **The** _____ **man walks with a cane.**

11. **His** _____ **hurts when he eats too much.**

12. **Please don't turn your** _____ **when I'm cutting your hair.**

Bill and Melinda Gates Foundation

Who has held the title of the richest person on earth for many years? It is Bill Gates. How did he make billions and billions of dollars? He did it by developing a software company. Have you heard of the company? It is Microsoft! What does Bill Gates do with all of his money?

In 2000, Bill and his wife, Melinda, started the Bill and Melinda Gates Foundation. The goals of the foundation are to improve healthcare and reduce extreme poverty in the world; and in the United States to expand educational opportunities and access to information technology.

The foundation is working on two devastating crises in Africa. First, it is supporting the development of a vaccine for Malaria which is the deadliest disease among African children. Second, the foundation is working with Botswana to combat the AIDS crisis by increasing access to HIV treatment and care.

In the United States, the foundation is working with dozens of states to ensure that high schools are educating students to the standards necessary to succeed. The foundation is working to ensure all Americans benefit from computer and the internet by helping public libraries with their computer and internet services.

Bill Gates is an American entrepreneur who is widely respected for his intelligence, foresight, and ambition. He began programming computers at the age of thirteen. Bill and Melinda have three children. Bill and his family live in one of the most expensive houses in the world. It is a modern earth-sheltered home, in the side of a hill, overlooking Lake Washington in the state of Washington.

Bill Gates not only developed a billion dollar software company but he and his wife started the Bill and Melinda Gates Foundation to improve healthcare, reduce poverty, and expand educational and technology opportunities around the world.

Comprehension Questions

Use la información en *Bill and Melinda Gates Foundation* para contestar las siguientes preguntas. Conteste cada pregunta con una oración completa.

1. Who is Bill Gates?

   _____

2. What are the four goals of the Bill and Melinda Gates Foundation?

   _____

   _____

3. What is the foundation doing in Africa?

   _____

   _____

4. What is the foundation doing in the United States?

   _____

   _____

5. When did Bill and Melinda start the foundation?

   _____

6. How did Bill Gates make all of his money?

   _____

7. When did Bill Gates start programming computers?

   _____

8. Bill and his family live in which state?

   _____

Sentences * Oraciones

Todas las oraciones deben tener cuatro cosas: un sujeto, un predicado (verbo), un signo de puntuación al final, y una mayúscula para comenzar la oración.

Escriba oraciones haciendo coincidir el sujeto con el predicado. La primera ya está hecha. Conserve esta página porque usará estas respuestas en las siguientes lecciones.

	Subject	Verb
1. *Ducks waddle.*	ducks	floats
2. _____	bird	ticks
3. _____	boys	buzz
4. _____	girl	crawls
5. _____	bug	flies
6. _____	feather	plays
7. _____	beavers	pulls
8. _____	ice	disagree
9. _____	ox	blows
10. _____	horse	swim
11. _____	clothes	melts
12. _____	bees	gallops
13. _____	candle	waddle
14. _____	wind	burns
15. _____	clock	hang

Vocabulary * Vocabulario

Encierre en un círculo la palabra que menos se relaciona con las otras tres.

1. whale   dolphin   seal   turtle

2. green   leaf   blue   red

3. adult   parent   girl   father

4. scales   arm   feathers   fur

5. robin   uncle   aunt   cousin

6. girl   aunt   uncle   mother

7. six   third   first   second

8. candles   hike   cake   present

9. drizzle   sleet   dust   rain

10. crutches   porches   stitches   bandages

11. eye   mouth   nose   leg

12. early   late   shoe   time

13. gold   grass   silver   bronze

14. backyard   kitchen   bedroom   bathroom

15. sink   tree   counter   shelf

16. shrimp   crab   bass   lobster

Answer Key * Las Respuestas

Fill in the Blanks * Llene el Espacio (page 65)

1. shoulder
2. heart
3. ankle
4. toenails
5. knuckles
6. perspires
7. throat
8. fingernails or fingernail
9. curls
10. old
11. stomach
12. head

Comprehension * Comprensión (page 67)

1. Bill Gates is the developer of Microsoft and has held the title as being the richest person on earth.
2. The goals of the foundation are to improve health care, reduce extreme poverty in the world, and to expand educational opportunities and access to information technology in the United States.
3. In Africa, it is working on a vaccine for Malaria and to increase access to HIV treatment and care.
4. In the United States, it is working to ensure high school students are being educated to the standards necessary to succeed. The foundation is also working with public libraries to ensure Americians benefit from computer and internet services.
5. The foundation was started in 2000.
6. Bill Gates made his money by developing a software company named Microsoft.
7. He began programming computers at the age of thirteen.
8. Bill and his family live in the state of Washington.

Sentences * Oraciones (page 68)

1.	Ducks waddle.	9.	Ox pulls.
2.	Birds fly.	10.	Horse gallops.
3.	Boys disagree.	11.	Clothes hang.
4.	Girl plays.	12.	Bees buzz.
5.	Bug crawls.	13.	Candle burns.
6.	Feather floats.	14.	Wind blows.
7.	Beavers swim.	15.	Clock ticks.
8.	Ice melts.		

Vocabulary * Vocabulario (page 69)

1.	turtle	5.	robin	9.	dust	13.	grass
2.	leaf	6.	uncle	10.	porches	14.	backyard
3.	girl	7.	six	11.	leg	15.	tree
4.	arm	8.	hike	12.	shoe	16.	bass

Lesson 11 * Lección 11
Vocabulary * Vocabulario
Math * Matemáticas

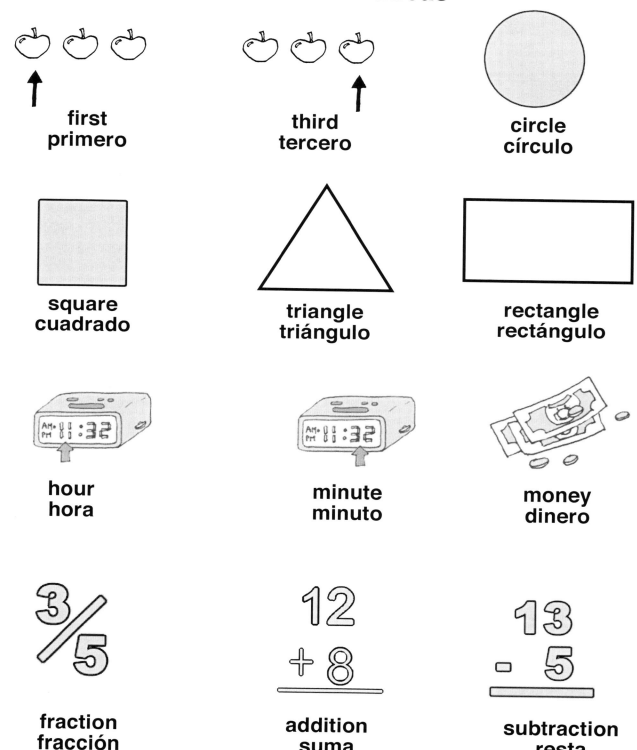

first
primero

third
tercero

circle
círculo

square
cuadrado

triangle
triángulo

rectangle
rectángulo

hour
hora

minute
minuto

money
dinero

fraction
fracción

addition
suma

subtraction
resta

Fill in the Blanks * Llene el Espacio

Llene cada espacio con una palabra de la página de vocabulario. Use la figura al final de la oración para ayudarse. Lea la oración con cuidado porque puede necesitar añadir una <u>s</u> o las letras <u>es</u> a la palabra del vocabulario.

1. A_____ has three corners.

2. The boy drew several _____ on his paper.

3. My sister earns _____ by mowing lawns .

4. Dinner will be ready in an _____ .

5. In first grade, children learn about _____ .

6. Sam was the _____ one home from school.

7. The boy uses his fingers to do his _____ .

8. We always visit my grandmother on the _____ Saturday of the month.

9. We will be at your house in ten _____ .

10. The girl had ten _____ problems for homework.

11. He colored the _____ blue.

12. The children sat in a _____ under the tree.

Iran

Iran is one of the world's oldest civilizations. For many years it was called Persia. Now, the official name is the Islamic Republic of Iran. It is a southwest Asian country located in the Middle East. Persian is the official language. The history of Iran covers thousands of years. Iran is a founding member of the United Nations.

Iran is the seventeenth-largest country in the world. It is just slightly larger than Alaska. Iran is one of the world's most mountainous countries. It has many rugged mountain ranges that separate areas from one another. Mount Damavand in Iran is the highest peak in the Middle East.

Most Iranians are Muslims; 90% belong to the Shi'a branch of Islam, the official state religion, and about 8% belong to the Sunni branch, mainly Kurds.

Iran has one of the highest urban-growth rates in the world. From 1950 to 2002, the urban proportion of the population increased from 27% to 60%. Tehran is the capital and largest city. More than half of the country's industry is based there. Industries include the manufacturing of cars, electronics and electrical equipment, military weaponry, textiles, sugar, cement, and chemical products.

Iran has a long history of art, music, architecture, poetry, philosophy, traditions, and ideology. It also has a long history of science. Iranians contributed significantly to the current understanding of astronomy, nature, medicine, mathematics, and philosophy. Persians first discovered Algebra, invented the windmill, and found medical uses for alcohol. Theoretical and computational sciences are rapidly developing in Iran. In late 2006, Iranian scientists cloned successfully a sheep, by somatic cell nuclear transfer.

The Persian Empire (Iran) established unprecedented principles of human rights in the 6th Century BC. Since then, the status of human rights in Iran has varied dramatically. Today, the violation of human rights by the Islamic Republic of Iran continues to be significant, despite many efforts by Iranian human right activists. Human rights in Iran regularly face the issues of governmental impunity, restricted freedom of speech, and gender inequality.

Iran is one of the oldest civilizations with a long history of art, music, architecture, poetry, philosophy, traditions, ideology, and science.

Comprehension Questions

Use la información en *Iran* para contestar las siguientes preguntas. Conteste cada pregunta con una oración completa.

1. What was Iran called for many years?

   _____

2. Iran is about the size of which state in the United States of America?

   _____

3. Where is Iran located?

   _____

4. What is the official language of Iran?

   _____

5. What religion are most Iranians?

   _____

6. What is the capital of Iran?

   _____

7. Name five things that are manufactured in Iran.

   _____

8. Name four areas of science that Iran has significantly contributed to.

   _____

9. When did Iran first establish principles of human rights and how have they recently been violated.

   _____

10. Look at the map. Is Tehran in the northern or southern part of the country?

    _____

Descriptive Sentences * Oraciones descriptivas

Llene la tabla con adjetivos y verbos. Los adjetivos son palabras que describen. Los sustantivos son personas, lugares, cosas, criaturas. Los verbos son palabras de acción. La primera ya está hecha.

Article	Adjective	Adjective	Noun	Verb
The	alert	triangular	ears	listen for danger
			arms	
A			candle	
			legs	
The			girl	
A			woman	
The			hat	
The			leaves	
A			nurse	

Ahora escriba las oraciones con la información de la tabla. La primera ya está hecha.

1. _The alert triangular ears listen for danger._

2. _____

3. _____

4. _____

5. _____

6. _____

7. _____

8. _____

9. _____

Sentences * Oraciones

Use las oraciones de la página 68 para hacer esta actividad. Añada la información sobre *dónde* a cada oración. Use las sugerencias del cuadro. La primera ya está hecha. Conserve esta página porque usará estas respuestas en la lección siguiente.

Where

1. *Ducks waddle in my backyard.*

2. _____

3. _____

4. _____

5. _____

6. _____

7. _____

8. _____

9. _____

10. _____

11. _____

12. _____

13. _____

14. _____

15. _____

Where
on the lake
in the kitchen
on the table
in my backyard
in the field
on the flowers
in the pond
in the sky
on the playground
on the leaf
outside
in the air
on the road
on the line
in the park

Answer Key * Las Respuestas

Fill in the Blanks * Llene el Espacio (page 72)

1. triangle	5. fractions	9. minutes
2. squares	6. first	10. subtraction
3. money	7. addition	11. rectangle
4. hour	8. last	12. circle

Comprehension * Comprensión (page 74)
1. Iran was called Persia.
2. Iran is slightly larger than Alaska.
3. Iran is located in the Middle East.
4. The official language is Persian.
5. Most Iranians are Muslims.
6. The capital of Iran is Tehran.
7. Cars, electronics, textiles, sugar, and cement are manufactured in Iran.
8. Iran has significantly contributed to the understanding of astronomy, nature, medicine, and mathematics.
9. Iran first established principles of human rights in the 6th Century BC. Human rights have been violated by restricted freedom of speech, gender inequality, and government impunity.
10. Tehran is in the northern part of Iran.

Descriptive Sentences * Oraciones descriptivas (page 75)
Answers will vary. Here are some examples.

Article	Adjective	Adjective	Noun	Verb
The	alert	triangular	ears	listen for danger
The	long	muscular	arms	caught the ball
A	small	stubby	candle	burned in the window
The	weak	wooden	legs	broke
The	smart	little	girl	read a book
A	tall	lean	woman	carried a backpack
The	old	ragged	hat	blew away
The	large	brown	leaves	fell from the tree
A	pretty	young	nurse	helped the man

1. The alert triangular ears listen for danger.
2. The long muscular arms caught the ball.
3. A small stubby candle burned in the window.
4. The weak wooden legs broke.
5. The smart little girl read a book.
6. A tall lean woman carried a backpack.
7. The old ragged hat blew away.
8. The large brown leaves fell from the tree.
9. A pretty young nurse helped the man.

Sentences * Oraciones (page 76)
Answers will vary. Here are some examples.
1. Ducks waddle in my backyard.
2. Birds fly in the sky.
3. Boys disagree on the playground.
4. Girl plays in the park.
5. Bug crawls on the leaf.
6. Feather floats in the air.
7. Beavers swim in the pond.
8. Ice melts on the lake.
9. Ox pulls in the field.
10. Horse gallops on the road.
11. Clothes hang on the line.
12. Bees buzz on the flowers.
13. Candle burns on the table.
14. Wind blows outside.
15. Clock ticks in the kitchen.

Lesson 12 * Lección 12

Vocabulary * Vocabulario

Verbs 2 * Verbos 2

Coloque las palabras de vocabulario en inglés en orden alfabético. Para hacerlo, escriba primero las palabras que comienzan con a, luego las que comienzan con b, después c, d, e, y así sucesivamente. Si dos palabras comienzan con la misma letra, entonces considere la siguiente letra y escriba la palabra que tenga la segunda letra más cercana al principio del alfabeto.

English	Spanish	Alphabetize
1. invite	invitar	1.
2. inspect	inspeccionar	2.
3. refill	rellenar	3.
4. respect	respetar	4.
5. relax	descansar	5.
6. agree	estar de acuerdo	6.
7. unpack	desempacar	7.
8. decide	decidir	8.
9. deliver	entregar	9.
10. begin	comenzar	10.
11. elect	elegir	11.
12. erase	borrar	12.
13. eject	expulsar	13.
14. scratch	rascar	14.
15. scream	gritar	15.

Fill in the Blanks * Llene el Espacio

Llene cada espacio con una palabra de la página de vocabulario. Use la palabra en español que se encuentra al final de la oración como ayuda. Lea la oración con cuidado porque puede necesitar añadir una s o las letras es a la palabra del vocabulario.

1. The store will _____ the dresses to our house. | entregar

2. We will _____ a new president at the next election. | elegir

3. The boy _____ when he sees the monster. | gritar

4. The inspectors will _____ the food on Friday. | inspeccionar

5. She _____ her suitcase and then goes to bed. | desempacar

6. My dog _____ because he has fleas. | rascar

7. It is important to _____ each other's differences. | respetar

8. He _____ the tape and puts in another one. | expulsar

9. We will _____ them to our house on Saturday. | invitar

10. The waiter _____ our glasses many times. | rellenar

11. The teacher _____ the board after school. | borrar

12. What did you _____to do? | decidir

13. We will _____ to clean the kitchen at ten o'clock. | comenzar

14. They like to _____ at the beach. | descansar

15. The boys could not _____ on how to solve the problem. | estar de acuerdo

Continents

How well do you know your geography? Did you know there are seven continents? In the United States of America, we say there are seven continents but in other parts of the world, they have a different answer. Look at the model below.

Model						
7 Continents	Antarctica	South America	North America	Europe	Asia	Africa	Australia
6 Continents	Antarctica	South America	North America	Eurasia	Africa	Australia
6 Continents	Antarctica	America	Europe	Asia	Africa	Australia
5 Continents	Antarctica	America	Eurasia	Africa	Australia
4 Continents	Antarctica	America	Africa-Eurasia	Australia

The seven continent model is taught in Western Europe, China, and most native English-speaking countries. The six continent model is taught in Russia, Eastern Europe, and Japan. The six continent combined America model is taught in Latin America, the Iberian Peninsula, Italy, Iran, and some parts of Europe. The five continent model is taught in the Iberian Peninsula and some other parts of Europe.

Since I am writing this in Huntington Beach, California, I will use the seven continent model for this comprehension page. Huntington Beach is a city in California and California is a state in the United States of America (USA) and the USA is a country on the continent of North America. Oh, what is a continent? A continent is one of the seven main land areas on earth.

Which is the largest continent? Asia is the largest continent. Which continent has the most people? Again, it is Asia. Which continent has the most countries? It is Africa. Do you know how many countries North America has? It has 23 countries. Really! I thought it only had three: Canada, USA, and Mexico. Don't forget the countries in Central America. They are part of North America, and the island countries in the Caribbean are also part of North America. Australia is the smallest continent. Which country has the least amount of people? That's right. Antarctica. Antarctica has a lot of penguins and a few visiting scientists.

When you hear the name of a country, do you know where it is located? Do you know which continent it is on? For example, do you remember which continent Iran is on? If not, look back in the previous lesson on page 73 to find out.

Comprehension Questions

Use la información en *Continents* para contestar las siguientes preguntas. Conteste cada pregunta con una oración completa.

1. How many continents are there?

   _____

2. What is a continent?

   _____

3. Does everyone agree on the number of continents?

   _____

4. Which is the largest continent?

   _____

5. Which continent has the most people?

   _____

6. Which continent has the most countries?

   _____

7. How many countries make up the North American continent?

   _____

8. Which continent has the most penguins?

   _____

9. Which continent is the farthest to the south?

   _____

10. Which continent would you like to visit? Tell why you chose that one.

   _____

Vocabulary * Vocabulario

Todas las palabras de la tabla siguiente pueden encontrarse en la historia *Continents*.

Vocabulary Word	Syllable # Clue	Semantic Clue
1. c _ _ _ _ _ _ _ _ _ _	4	the ability to understand
2. p _ _ _ _ _ _	2	a bird from the antarctic region, with webbed feet and flippers for swimming
3. t _ _ _ _ _	1	the past tense of teach
4. i _ _ _ _ _	2	land smaller than a continent and surrounded by water
5. c _ _ _ _ _ _ _	3	one of the seven main land areas on earth
6. p _ _ _ _ _ _ _ _	4	a long piece of land almost completely surrounded by water
7. n _ _ _ _ _	2	belonging to a person because of the place where the person was born
8. g _ _ _ _ _ _ _ _	4	the study of the surface of the earth and how it is divided into continents, countries, seas and other parts
9. A _ _ _ _ _ _ _ _ _	4	a continent around the South Pole
10. C _ _ _ _ _ _ _ _	4	a sea in the Atlantic Ocean
11. l _ _ _ _ _	1	smallest in amount, size or importance
12. s _ _ _ _ _ _ _ _	3	an expert in science
13. l _ _ _ _ _	2	to find out where something is
14. p _ _ _ _ _ _ _	3	before

Sentences * Oraciones

Use las oraciones de la página 76 para hacer esta actividad. Añada una palabra descriptiva acerca del sujeto en cada oración. Use las sugerencias del cuadro. Después de haber añadido el adjetivo, añada un artículo al principio de las oraciones que lo necesiten. Las primeras dos ya están hechas. Guarde esta página porque usará estas respuestas en la siguiente lección.

Where

1. *Four ducks waddle in the park.* _____
2. *A red bird flies in the sky.* _____
3. _____
4. _____
5. _____
6. _____
7. _____
8. _____
9. _____
10. _____
11. _____
12. _____
13. _____
14. _____
15. _____

busy

strong

two

graceful

red

thick

black

four

wet

cold

blue

antique

scented

several

small

Answer Key * Las Respuestas

Alphabetizing * Colocar en orden alfabético (page 78)

1.	agree	5.	eject	9.	invite	13.	scratch
2.	begin	6.	elect	10.	refill	14.	scream
3.	decide	7.	erase	11.	relax	15.	unpack
4.	deliver	8.	inspect	12.	respect		

Fill in the Blanks * Llene el Espacio (page 79)

1.	deliver	6.	scratches	11.	erases
2.	elect	7.	respect	12.	decide
3.	screams	8.	ejects	13.	begin
4.	inspect	9.	invite	14.	relax
5.	unpacks	10.	refills	15.	agree

Comprehension * Comprensión (page 81)

1. There are seven continents.
2. A continent is one of the seven main land areas on earth.
3. Everyone does not agree on the number of continents.
4. Asia is the largest continent.
5. Asia has the most people.
6. Africa has the most countries.
7. North America has 23 countries.
8. Antarctica has the most penguins.
9. Antarctica is the farthest to the south.
10. I would like to visit Europe because it is made up of many countries which I would like to visit.
   (Answers will vary for #10.)

Vocabulary * Vocabulario (page 82)

1.	comprehension	8.	geography
2.	penquin	9.	Antarctica
3.	taught	10.	Caribbean
4.	island	11.	least
5.	continent	12.	scientist
6.	peninsula	13.	locate
7.	native	14.	previous

Sentences * Oraciones (page 83)

Answers will vary. Here are some examples.

1. Four ducks waddle in the park.
2. A red bird flies in the sky.
3. Several boys disagree on the playground.
4. A small girl plays in the park.
5. A blue bug crawls on the leaf.
6. Two feathers float in the air.
7. Busy beavers swim in the pond.
8. The thick ice melts on the lake.
9. The strong ox pulls in the field.
10. The graceful horse gallops on the road.
11. The wet clothes hang on the line.
12. The black bees buzz on the flowers.
13. The scented candle burns on the table.
14. Cold wind blows outside.
15. The antique clock ticks in the kitchen.

Lesson 13 * Lección 13

Vocabulary * Vocabulario

Numbers * Números

60
sixty
sesenta

70
seventy
setenta

80
eighty
ochenta

90
ninety
noventa

100
one hundred
cien

101
one hundred one
ciento uno

115
one hundred fifteen
ciento quince

120
one hundred twenty
ciento veinte

125
one hundred twenty-five
ciento veinticinco

150
one hundred fifty
ciento cincuenta

200
two hundred
doscientos

500
five hundred
quinientos

Fill in the Blanks * Llene el Espacio

Llene cada espacio con una palabra de la página de vocabulario. Use el número al final de la oración como ayuda.

1. My grandmother likes to drive ____ miles an hour. **60**

2. The farmer sold _____ pigs last year. **150**

3. Tom read _____ pages in his book last night. **90**

4. My sister weighs _____ pounds. **101**

5. We drove _____ miles on our trip. **500**

6. The little girl ate _____ jellybeans. **125**

7. My mother is _____ years old. **80**

8. Every day my sister drives _____ miles. **120**

9. The children have been in school _____ days. **100**

10. The boy counted _____ trees in the park. **115**

11. My uncle will be _____ years old on Saturday. **70**

12. The farmer planted _____ apple trees. **200**

The Nile River

The Nile River is the longest river in the world. On which continent is it located? No, not South America, that's the Amazon River. The Amazon River is the second longest river in the world. The Nile is located on the continent of Africa. Africa is the second largest continent but is the continent with the most countries. Where is the Nile River on Africa and which countries does it pass through?

The Nile River is 4,184 miles long. It is a northern flowing river which runs along the eastern part of Africa from Uganda to Ethiopia, winding through nine countries. The Nile River is often associated with Egypt; but it also touches Ethiopia, Zaire, Kenya, Uganda, Tanzania, Rwanda, Burundi, and Sudan. It has two major tributaries the White Nile and the Blue Nile. The source of the Nile is Lake Victoria, the largest lake in Africa. This lake has many feeder rivers, the most distant coming from the Nyungwe Forest in Rwanda. The Nile ends in a large delta that empties into the Mediterranean Sea. A delta is a triangle-shaped piece of land at the mouth of a large river. The delta is formed by deposits of soil and sand at the mouth of the river. Cairo, Egypt, near the mouth of the Nile, is the largest city on the river.

The Nile River has played an important role in the history of Egypt. It has been the lifeline for Egyptian culture since the Stone Age. Cities and civilizations grew up along the banks of the Nile because of the fertile soil the river produces. The Nile River has provided drinking water, irrigation for farming, a convenient and efficient way of transportation, as well as papyrus reeds for paper and building materials from ancient to modern times.

A good way to view the Nile River would be to cruise the river on a cruise ship, a traditional wooden sailing boat called a felucca, or on one of the many "floating hotels." You'll be able to get a good view of the countryside and be able to visit different cities and towns. If you travel on a "floating hotel" you can enjoy the scenery from your own private sun deck. Keep your eyes peeled for Nile crocodiles. These animals have been part of the Egyptian culture since the first Egyptians settled along the banks of the Nile. The crocodiles are about four meters in length. They make their nests along the banks of the river, where the female can lay up to 60 eggs at one time. In three months, the babies will be born and will stay with their mother for at least two years before reaching maturity. Bon Voyage!

Comprehension Questions

Use la información en *The Nile River* para contestar las siguientes preguntas. Conteste cada pregunta con una oración completa.

1. How long is the Nile River?

   _____

2. Where is the Nile River located?

   _____

3. What is the second longest river in the world?

   _____

4. Which direction does the Nile River flow?

   _____

5. How many countries does the Nile River touch?

   _____

6. Name the two major tributaries to the Nile River.

   _____

7. What sea does the Nile empty into?

   _____

8. What is a delta?

   _____

9. What is the largest city on the Nile and in which country is it located?

   _____

10. What famous culture grew up along the Nile River?

   _____

Sentences * Oraciones

Use las oraciones de la página 83 para hacer esta actividad. Añada la información sobre *cuándo* al principio de cada oración. Use las sugerencias del cuadro. La primera ya está hecha.

When

1. <u>Every morning</u> *four ducks waddle in my backyard.*

2. _____

3. _____

4. _____

5. _____

6. _____

7. _____

8. _____

9. _____

10. _____

11. _____

12. _____

13. _____

14. _____

15. _____

When
all day long
after the rain
in the afternoon
every day
Monday
Saturday
during the day
in the morning
at night
every morning
every evening
after the storm
during the storm
at recess
at noon

Vocabulary * Vocabulario

Trace un círculo alrededor de 18 animales.

robin	shirt	squirrel
circle	snake	scratch
falcon	puddle	parrot
front	jungle	bear
crocodile	turtle	shrub
beaver	inspect	alligator
jacket	harmless	great
hawk	eagle	owl
boa constrictor	kind	lizard
ox	horse	whale

En la tabla a continuación, escriba los dieciocho animales bajo el grupo correcto de animales.

Mammal	Reptile	Bird

Answer Key * Las Respuestas

Fill in the Blanks * Llene el Espacio (page 86)

1. sixty
2. one hundred fifty
3. ninety
4. one hundred one
5. five hundred
6. one hundred twenty-five
7. eighty
8. one hundred twenty
9. one hundred
10. one hundred fifteen
11. seventy
12. two hundred

Comprehension * Comprensión (page 88)

1. The Nile River is 4,184 miles long.
2. The Nile is located on the continent of Africa.
3. The second longest river is the Amazon River.
4. The Nile flows to the north.
5. The Nile River touches 9 countries.
6. The two major tributaries are the White Nile and the Blue Nile.
7. The Nile empties into the Mediterranean Sea.
8. A delta is a triangle-shaped piece of land at the mouth of a large river and is formed by deposits of soil and sand.
9. The largest city on the Nile is Cairo, located in Egypt.
10. The Egyptian culture grew up along the Nile River.

Sentences * Oraciones (page 89)

Answers will vary. **Here are some examples.**

1. Every morning four ducks waddle in my backyard.
2. On Saturday a red bird flies in the sky.
3. At recess several boys disagree on the playground.
4. At noon a small girl plays in the park.
5. After the rain a blue bug crawls on the leaf.
6. In the morning two feathers float in the air.
7. All day long the busy beavers swim in the pond.
8. In the afternoon the thick ice melts on the lake.
9. During the day a strong ox pulls in the field.
10. After the storm a graceful horse gallops on the road.
11. On Monday the wet clothes hand on the line.
12. Every evening the black bees buzz on the flowers.
13. At night the scented candle burns on the table.
14. During the storm a cold wind blows outside.
15. Every day the antique clock ticks in the kitchen.

Vocabulary * Vocabulario (page 90)

robin	beaver	ox	eagle	parrot	owl
falcon	hawk	snake	horse	bear	lizard
crocodile	boa constrictor	turtle	squirrel	alligator	whale

Mammal	Reptile	Bird
beaver	crocodile	robin
ox	boa constrictor	falcon
horse	snake	hawk
squirrel	turtle	eagle
bear	alligator	parrot
whale	lizard	owl

Lesson 14 * Lección 14

Vocabulary * Vocabulario

Describing Words * Palabras de descripción

Coloque las palabras de vocabulario en inglés en orden alfabético. Para hacerlo, escriba primero las palabras que comienzan con <u>a</u>, luego las que comienzan con <u>b</u>, después <u>c</u>, <u>d</u>, <u>e</u>, y así sucesivamente. Si dos palabras comienzan con la misma letra, entonces considere la siguiente letra y escriba la palabra que tenga la segunda letra más cercana al principio del alfabeto.

English	Spanish	Alphabetize
1. rocky	rocoso	1.
2. sleepy	soñoliento	2.
3. windy	ventoso	3.
4. dusty	polvoso	4.
5. unmade	sin hacer	5.
6. uneven	disparejo	6.
7. extra	adicional	7.
8. kind	tipo	8.
9. mild	templado	9.
10. old	viejo	10.
11. most	la mayoría	11.
12. pretty	bonito	12.
13. heavy	pesado	13.
14. harmless	inofensivo	14.

Fill in the Blanks * Llene el Espacio

Llene cada espacio con una palabra de la página de vocabulario. Use la palabra en español que se encuentra al final de la oración como ayuda.

1. Mom bought _____ party dresses for the girls. | **bonito**

2. The _____ man had a hole in his pocket. | **viejo**

3. The trail down the mountain was _____ and slippery. | **rocoso**

4. This stretch of the road is _____ and bumpy. | **disparejo**

5. In California we have _____ winters. | **templado**

6. That box is too _____ to lift. | **pesada**

7. The old vacant house was _____ and dirty. | **polvosa**

8. _____ birds can fly. | **La mayoría**

9. What _____ of cake do you want to make? | **tipo**

10. That big yellow dog is _____. | **inofensivo**

11. The _____ boy could not keep his eyes open. | **soñoliento**

12. His bed is always _____. | **sin hacer**

13. Here are some _____ napkins for the picnic. | **adicional**

14. Saturday was a cold and _____ day. | **ventoso**

Iraq

Iraq is the 58th largest country in the world. It is about the size of California. It is a country in Southwest Asia. It shares borders with the countries of Kuwait and Saudi Arabia to the south, Jordan to the west, Syria to the northwest, Turkey to the north, and Iran to the east. It has a narrow section of coastline on the Persian Gulf.

Much of Iraq is desert, but the land between the two major rivers (Euphrates and Tigris) is fertile. The northern part of the country is mostly mountainous. The climate is mostly mild to cool winters with hot, dry summers. The mountainous regions have cold winters with heavy snows which can cause extensive flooding. The capital city of Baghdad is situated in the center of the country along the banks of the Tigris River.

Iraq ranks second in the world behind Saudi Arabia in oil reserves. Up to 90 percent of the country still remains unexplored. These unexplored regions could yield up to billions of barrels of oil. Only about 2,000 oil wells have been drilled in Iraq compared to about one million wells in Texas.

Historically, Iraq was known as Mesopotamia. This land was home to the world's first know civilization. The early cultures of this area produced the earliest writing and some of the first sciences, mathematics, laws and philosophies in the world, making the region the center of what is known as the "Cradle of Civilization." Ancient Mesopotamian civilization dominated other civilizations of its time. In the sixth century BC, the region became part of the Persian Empire for nearly four centuries before it was conquered by Alexander the Great and remained under Greek rule for nearly two centuries. Beginning in the seventh century AD, Islam spread to what is now Iraq. Baghdad was the leading city of the Arab and Muslim world for five centuries.

Most Iraqis are Arabs. The other major ethnic group is Kurds. The Kurds differ from the Arabs in many ways, including culture, history, clothing, and language. Arabic and Kurdish are the official languages. Most Iraqis are either Shi'te or Sunni Muslims made up of mostly Arabs and Kurds.

The area of Iraq has been civilized for centuries beginning BC (before Christ.) The civilizations of this area have contributed to producing the earliest writing and some of the first sciences, mathematics, laws and philosophies in the world.

Comprehension Questions

Use la información en *Iraq* para contestar las siguientes preguntas. Conteste cada pregunta con una oración completa.

1. How big is Iraq?

   _____

2. Where is Iraq located?

   _____

3. Name two types of land regions in Iraq?

   _____

4. Name the two major rivers in Iraq.

   _____

5. What is the capital of Iraq?

   _____

6. What is a major natural resource of Iraq?

   _____

7. Long, long ago, Iraq was known as what?

   _____

8. Why is the area of Iraq know as the "Cradle of Civilization"?

   _____

9. What are the two major ethnic groups in Iraq?

   _____

10. Most Iraqis belong to which of the two Muslim groups?

   _____

Sentence Practice * Práctica de oraciones

Lea cada oración. Subraye el sujeto sencillo y encierre el verbo sencillo en un cuadro. Cada oración debe tener un verbo (una palabra de acción) y un sujeto (persona, cosa, lugar o criatura que realize la acción). Encuentre la palabra de acción primero y luego encuentre el sujeto que está realizando la acción. La primera ya está hecha.

1. The little <u>girl</u> in the red dress `runs` quickly down the street.

2. The pink dresses hang in the front closet.

3. The cat's eyes close in the bright sunshine.

4. The boy hid the enormous egg under the porch.

5. My mother's ankles swell every afternoon.

6. The children laugh at the funny clown.

7. The homeless person sleeps under the bridge.

8. On the beach, the crabs crawl quickly on the sand.

9. In the kitchen, my dad cooks breakfast for everyone.

10. At the pool, the little boy in the red trunks jumped into the deep end.

11. On Thursdays, my mom goes grocery shopping.

12. On Saturdays, my dad jogs at the park.

13. My uncle spilled milk on the new carpet.

14. The old woman walks with a cane.

15. The blue shirt shrank in the hot dryer.

16. The little boy winks at the pretty girl.

17. In his bedroom, the boy unpacks his suitcase.

Prefixes and Suffixes * Prefijos y sufijos

Prefixes   **Suffixes**

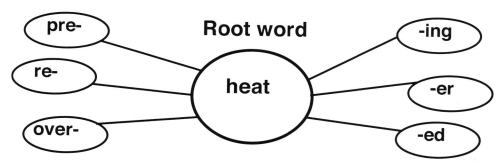

Escriba seis palabras nuevas añadiendo los prefijos y sufijos a la palabra raíz. La primera ya está hecha.

1. _____preheat_____   4. _____

2. _____   5. _____

3. _____   6. _____

Use una de las palabras nuevas en cada oración.

7. Every winter our _____ bill is very high.

8. Mom _____ the soup in a small pan.

9. For supper we will _____ the leftovers.

10. You need to _____ the oven before baking the cookies.

11. You will need to stop the car if the engine begins to ____ .

12. Dad fixed the _____ and now our house is warm.

Add a prefix and a suffix to the rootword to fill in the blank.

13. Mom is _____ the oven before she bakes.

14. The car's engine _____ when we went up the steep hill.

15. Dad _____ the leftovers for dinner.

16. He _____ the food and now it is burnt.

Answer Key * Las Respuestas

Alphabetizing * Colocar en orden alfabético (page 92)

1.	dusty	5.	kind	9.	pretty	13.	unmade
2.	extra	6.	mild	10.	rocky	14.	windy
3.	harmless	7.	most	11.	sleepy		
4.	heavy	8.	old	12.	uneven		

Fill in the Blanks * Llene el Espacio (page 93)

1. pretty
2. old
3. rocky
4. uneven
5. mild
6. heavy
7. dusty
8. Most
9. kind
10. harmless
11. sleepy
12. unmade
13. extra
14. windy

Comprehension * Comprensión (page 95)

1. Iraq is about the size of California.
2. Iraq is located in Southwest Asia.
3. There are desert and mountainous regions in Iraq.
4. The two major rivers in Iraq are the Euphrates and the Tigris rivers.
5. Baghdad is the capital of Iraq.
6. Oil is the major natural resource.
7. Historically, Iraq was known as Mesopotamia.
8. It is known as the "Cradle of Civilization" because the early cultures of this area produced the earliest writings and the first sciences, mathematics, laws, and philosophies.
9. The two major ethnic groups are Arabs and Kurds.
10. Most Iraqis are either Shi'te or Sunni Muslims.

Sentences Practice * Práctica de oraciones (page 96)

	Subject	Action Word (Verb)
1.	girl	runs
2.	dresses	hang
3.	eyes	cose
4.	boy	hid
5.	ankles	swell
6.	children	laugh
7.	person	sleeps
8.	crabs	crawl
9.	dad	cooks
10.	boy	jumped
11.	mom	goes
12.	dad	jogs
13.	uncle	spilled
14.	woman	walks
15.	shirt	shrank
16.	boy	winks
17.	boy	unpacks

Prefixes and Suffixes * Prefijos y sufijos (page 97)

1.	preheat	5.	heater	9.	reheat	13.	preheating
2.	reheat	6.	heated	10.	preheat	14.	overheated
3.	overheat	7.	heating	11.	overheat	15.	reheated
4.	heating	8.	heated	12.	heater	16.	overheated

Lesson 15 * Lección 15

Vocabulary * Vocabulario

Describing Words 2 * Palabras de descripción 2

Coloque las palabras de vocabulario en inglés en orden alfabético. Para hacerlo, escriba primero las palabras que comienzan con a, luego las que comienzan con b, después c, d, e, y así sucesivamente. Si dos palabras comienzan con la misma letra, entonces considere la siguiente letra y escriba la palabra que tenga la segunda letra más cercana al principio del alfabeto.

English	Spanish	Alphabetize
1. softly	suavemente	1.
2. gladly	con gusto	2.
3. inside	interior	3.
4. before	antes	4.
5. front	frente	5.
6. perfect	perfecto	6.
7. among	entre	7.
8. early	temprano	8.
9. useful	útil	9.
10. open	abierto	10.
11. enough	suficiente	11.
12. slowest	el más lento	12.
13. fastest	el más rápido	13.
14. spoonful	cucharada	14.

Fill in the Blanks * Llene el Espacio

Llene cada espacio con una palabra de la página de vocabulario. Use la palabra en español que se encuentra al final de la oración como ayuda.

1. All of the _____ doors are painted blue. | interior

2. He _____ gave the crutches back to the doctor. | con gusto

3. Every morning he puts a _____ of medicine in his glass of water. | cucharada

4. That teacher's classroom door is always _____ . | abierto

5. The shoes are a _____ size for me. | perfecto

6. Sam will paint the _____ door red. | frente

7. A down feather landed _____ on her nose. | suavemente

8. There is a wolf _____ the sheep! | entre

9. A snail is one of the _____ creatures. | el más

10. My sister goes to bed _____ every night. | temprano

11. Try to find something _____ to do. | útil

12. Do you have _____ candles for the birthday cake? | suficiente

13. That girl is the _____ runner in our class. | el más rápido

14. In math class, we learn multiplication _____ division. | antes

Amelia Earhart

What happened to Amelia Earhart? Who was Amelia Earhart? She was a famous aviator. What is an aviator? An aviator is an airplane pilot.

Amelia Earhart was born in Atchison, Kansas in 1897. She was a tomboy who loved to climb trees, hunt for rats with a rifle, and belly slam her sled down a snowy hill. In 1920 she took her first airplane flight. As soon as the plane left the ground, she knew she wanted to become a pilot. A few days later she took her first flying lesson and six months later she bought her own plane. In 1921 she got her U.S. flying license; in 1922 she set the women's altitude record of 14,000 feet; and in 1923 she received her international pilot's license. There were only 15 other women in the world to have this license.

In 1928, Amelia was the first woman to fly across the Atlantic Ocean. She did not fly the plane. Instead, she was a passenger. Originally, Amy Guest, a wealthy 55 year-old American, had bought the plane to make the flight. She wanted to be the first woman to fly across the Atlantic; but then she decided it was too dangerous, so Amelia was asked to do it. Amelia's flight across the ocean took almost 21 hours. After the flight Amelia became a media sensation. She and the two pilots were given a ticker tape parade down Broadway in New York City. President Coolidge called to congratulate her on the flight.

Earhart participated in flying competitions and became a member of the Ninety Nines, an organization of women pilots providing support and advancing the cause of women in aviation. She also published a book about her flight across the Atlantic Ocean and did many lecture tours and endorsements for products. In 1932 she became the first woman to fly solo across the Atlantic Ocean. After this, she did other solo flights to different destinations.

On May 21, 1937 Amelia took off from Oakland, California with her navigator Fed Noonan to fly around the world. July 2, 1937 was the last time anyone received radio contact from her as she flew over the Pacific Ocean. Nobody knows what happened to Amelia and Fed. Even though her plane has never been found, most people believe the plane ran out of gas and crashed into the ocean. Others think they landed and were captured by the Japanese.

Guided by her husband who was a publicist, Amelia made headlines throughout her aviation career in an era when the public was fascinated with flying.

Comprehension Questions

Use la información en *Amelia Earhart* para contestar las siguientes preguntas. Conteste cada pregunta con una oración completa.

1. Who was Amelia Earhart?

   _____

2. What is an aviator?

   _____

3. In what state was Amelia born?

   _____

4. What did Amelia like to do when she was a little girl?

   _____

5. When did Amelia become interested in flying?

   _____

6. What did Amelia do in 1928?

   _____

7. What did Amelia do in 1932?

   _____

8. What did Amelia do in 1937?

   _____

9. What do you think happened to Amelia?

   _____

10. What is a publicist?

    _____

Sentence Practice * Práctica de oraciones

En esta página, cada oración necesita una parte de sujeto, una parte de acción y una parte que indica dónde. Lea cada oración y luego decida cuál parte falta. Si falta el sujeto, escribe S al final de la oración. Si falta la parte de la acción, escriba V (por verbo). Si falta la parte que indica dónde, escriba W. Después escriba la palabra o las palabras que faltan. La primera ya está hecha.

1. The small girl ___*played*___ in the park.   __V__

2. The bees buzz near _____.   _____

3. Pam _____ a new dress at the shop.   _____

4. The boys _____ in the pool.   _____

5. _____ falls down the steps.   _____

6. _____ crashes into the tree.   _____

7. _____ the children read many books.   _____

8. Dad _____ in the kitchen.   _____

9. The artist _____ in his studio.   _____

10. Outside _____ blow down the street.   _____

11. He _____ his keys in the car.   _____

12. Your purple _____ are under the bed.   _____

13. At the beach, many people _____.   _____

14. The dog _____ in the backyard.   _____

15. The turtle sits _____.   _____

16. The girl _____ milk on the table.   _____

Prefixes and Suffixes * Prefijos y sufijos

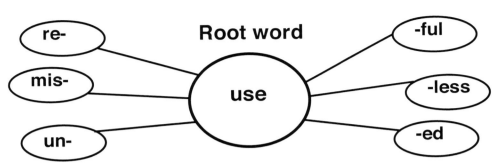

Prefixes

Suffixes

re-

mis-

un-

Root word

use

-ful

-less

-ed

Escriba seis palabras nuevas añadiendo los prefijos y sufijos a la palabra raíz. La primera ya está hecha.

1. _____reuse_____   4. _____

2. _____   5. _____

3. _____   6. _____

Use una de las palabras nuevas en cada oración.

7. This tool is _____ for all kinds of jobs.

8. My brother bought a _____ car on Saturday.

9. We will save these boxes and _____ them later.

10. Do not _____ the tool or it may break.

11. My sister wants a brand new _____ computer.

12. This engine can not be fixed so it is _____ .

Add a prefix and a suffix to the rootword to fill in the blank.

13. He _____ his toy and it finally broke.

14. My mother washed and _____ the plastic silverware.

15. This new building is still vacant and _____ .

Answer Key * Las Respuestas

Alphabetizing * Colocar en orden alfabético (page 99)

1.	among	5.	fastest	9.	open	13.	spoonful
2.	before	6.	front	10.	perfect	14.	useful
3.	early	7.	gladly	11.	slowest		
4.	enough	8.	inside	12.	softly		

Fill in the Blanks * Llene el Espacio (page 100)

1. inside
2. gladly
3. spoonful
4. open
5. perfect
6. front
7. softly
8. among
9. slowest
10. early
11. useful
12. enough
13. fastest
14. before

Comprehension * Comprensión (page 102)

1. Amelia Earhart was a famous aviator.
2. An aviator is an airplane pilot.
3. Amelia was born in Kansas.
4. Amelia liked to climb trees, hunt with a rifle, and sled down snowy hills.
5. Amelia became interested in flying in 1920.
6. In 1928, Amelia was the first woman to fly across the Atlantic Ocean.
7. In 1932, she was the first woman to fly solo across the Atlantic Ocean.
8. In 1937, she and her navigator started to fly around the world, but were never heard from again.
9. I think her plane crashed into the ocean.
10. A publicist is a press agent.

Sentences Practice * Práctica de oraciones (page 103) Answers will vary except for the parts of speech. Here are some examples.

Subject	Verb	Where
1.	played	
2.		the flowers
3.	bought	
4.	swam	
5. Tom		
6. Mary		
7.		in the library
8.	cooks	
9.	paints	
10. leaves		
11.	locked	
12. slippers		
13.	surf	
14.	digs	
15.		on the rock
16.	spilled	

Prefixes and Suffixes * Prefijos y sufijos (page 104)

1.	reuse	5.	useless	9.	reuse	13.	misused
2.	misuse	6.	used	10.	misuse	14.	reused
3.	unuse	7.	useful	11.	unused	15.	unused
4.	useful	8.	used	12.	useless		

Lesson 16 * Lección 16

Vocabulary * Vocabulario

Verbs 3 * Verbos 3

Coloque las palabras de vocabulario en inglés en orden alfabético. Para hacerlo, escriba primero las palabras que comienzan con a, luego las que comienzan con b, después c, d, e, y así sucesivamente. Si dos palabras comienzan con la misma letra, entonces considere la siguiente letra y escriba la palabra que tenga la segunda letra más cercana al principio del alfabeto.

English	Spanish	Alphabetize
1. shrink	encoger	1.
2. split	partir	2.
3. splash	salpicar	3.
4. spray	rociar	4.
5. build	construir	5.
6. throw	lanzar	6.
7. squeeze	apretar	7.
8. squirt	echar un chorro	8.
9. walk	caminar	9.
10. talk	hablar	10.
11. disagree	estar en desacuerdo	11.
12. discuss	hablar de	12.
13. enjoy	disfrutar	13.
14. entertain	entretener	14.

Fill in the Blanks * Llene el Espacio

Llene cada espacio con una palabra de la página de vocabulario. Use la palabra en español que se encuentra al final de la oración como ayuda. Lea la oración con cuidado porque puede necesitar añadir una s o las letras es a la palabra del vocabulario.

1. The woman _____ to the girls about safety. | **hablar**

2. He _____ going camping for his vacation. | **disfrutar**

3. The small boy _____ through the window. | **apretar**

4. The girl _____ the problem with her friend. | **hablar de**

5. My uncle _____ the logs with his ax. | **partir**

6. Do not _____ your sister with the hose. | **echar un chorro**

7. The boy _____ with his father. | **estar en desacuerdo**

8. Dad _____ the windows with water. | **rociar**

9. She _____ home in the drizzle. | **caminar**

10. They plan to _____ a subway under the city. | **construir**

11. The clowns will _____ the children at the party. | **entretener**

12. Your clothes might _____ in the dryer. | **encoger**

13. The children jump and _____ in the pool. | **salpicar**

14. The boy _____ the football to his mother. | **lanzar**

The Amazon River

Did you know that dolphins live in the Amazon River? The Amazon River is the second longest river in the world, but the largest river in terms of volume with six times greater total water flow than the next six largest rivers combined. The Amazon River also has the largest watershed in the world and the most tributaries. The Amazon and its tributaries wind through the northern half of South America flowing through the countries of Peru, Bolivia, Venezuela, Colombia, Ecuador, and Brazil before emptying into the Atlantic Ocean 6,437 kilometers (4,000 miles) from its headwaters high in the Andes mountains of Peru. This huge watershed includes the largest tropical rainforest in the world as well as areas of dry grassland.

Many animals live in the Amazon. The Boto dolphins lives in the Amazon River. These dolphins are vulnerable because of the continued destruction of the rainforest environment. The major threats to their survival are pollution, deforestation, entanglement in fishing nets, and competition for fish with humans. The carnivorous fish, Piranhas, also live in the Amazon. They swim in large schools and may attack livestock and humans. In 1981, 300 people were killed by a school of piranhas when their boat capsized. With their sharp teeth, piranhas can strip the flesh from bones in just a few minutes. But only a few species of piranhas attack humans, and many are solely fish-eaters, and do not swim in schools. The Anaconda is the largest snake in the world and is found in shallow waters in the Amazon basin. It spends much of its time in the water with just its nostrils above the surface. Thousands of species of fish, crabs, and turtles also live in the Amazon River.

The Amazon is home to a variety of Indian cultures who have a great deal of knowledge about the Amazon rainforest. As settlement brings changes to the forest, these cultural groups are also changing, and the lessons they have gained through thousands of years of living within the rainforest are in danger of being lost. Scientists are trying to learn from the native people of the Amazon about the rainforest plants and animals that may hold cures to many diseases.

The Amazon River, with its huge watershed, includes the largest tropical rainforest in the world. The destruction of the forest as settlers clear the land for farming and companies harvest trees for lumber is believed to be contributing to the problem of global warming. It's important to preserve the Amazon River and its huge watershed that includes the largest rainforest in the world!

Comprehension Questions

Use la información en *The Amazon River* para contestar las siguientes preguntas. Conteste cada pregunta con una oración completa.

1. Where is the Amazon River?

   _____

2. What is a watershed? (Use a dictionary to find your answer.)

   _____

3. Where is the largest tropical rainforest?

   _____

4. What kind dolphins live in the Amazon?

   _____

5. Name four threats to the river dolphins.

   _____

6. Name two other animals that live in the Amazon River.

   _____

7. What ocean does the Amazon empty into?

   _____

8. In which country does the Amazon begin?

   _____

9. What are tributaries?

   _____

10. Name two things that are destroying the Amazon Rainforest.

    _____

Vocabulary * Vocabulario

Todas las palabras de la tabla siguiente pueden encontrarse en la historia _The Amazon River_.

Vocabulary Word	Syllable # Clue	Semantic Clue
1. l _ _ _ _ _ _ _ _	2	farm animals such as cattle, horses, pigs, or sheep
2. c _ _ _ _ _ _	2	the ideas, skills, arts, tools, food, and way of life of a certain people at a certain time
3. e _ _ _ _ _ _ _ _ _ _	4	to be trapped
4. p _ _ _ _ _ _ _	2	to protect from harm
5. n _ _ _ _ _ _ _	2	the two openings in the nose through which a person smells and breathes
6. r _ _ _ _ _ _ _ _ _	3	an area dense with trees and other plants that has a heavy rainfall all year round
7. v _ _ _ _ _ _ _ _ _	4	able to be hurt, destroyed or attacked
8. t _ _ _ _ _ _ _ _	4	a stream or river that flows into a larger one
9. s _ _ _ _ _	1	a large group of fish swimming together
10. w _ _ _ _ _ _ _ _	3	all the land that is drained by a river and by all the streams flowing into the river
11. t _ _ _ _ _ _ _	3	having to do with the area near the equator between the Tropic of Cancer and the Topic of Capricorn
12. d _ _ _ _ _ _	2	a mammal that lives in water and has a long snout
13. n _ _ _ _ _ _	2	a person who was born in a certain place or region
14. c _ _ _ _ _ _ _ _ _ _	4	feeding on other animals

Compound Sentences * Oraciones compuestas

Una oración compuesta tiene dos o más cláusulas independientes unidas por una conjunction coordinadora. Una cláusula independiente tiene un sujeto y un verbo y puede sostenerse sola (oración sencilla). Las palabras siguientes son conjunciones coordinadoras: *and*, *but* y *or*. Lea las siguientes oraciones compuestas y subraye la conjunction en cada oración.

1. **The children ate breakfast and then they did their chores.**

2. **I will fold the clothes but I will not put them away.**

3. **You may go to your friend's house or your friend can come here.**

4. **Mom will sew the pants and Jan will iron the skirts.**

5. **Dad will wash the walls but he will not mop the floor.**

6. **Mom can cook the fish or Dad can grill the steaks.**

7. **Cats like to sleep and kittens like to play.**

Ahora escriba sus propias oraciones compuestas. Asegúrese de que cada oración tenga una de las siguientes conjunciones: *and*, *but*, *or*. Asegúrese de que cada oración tenga dos cláusulas independiente. Cada cláusula debe tener un sujeto y un verbo y poder sostenerse sola.

8. _____

9. _____

10. _____

11. _____

12. _____

Answer Key * Las Respuestas

Alphabetizing * Colocar en orden alfabético (page 106)

1.	build	5.	entertain	9.	spray	13.	throw
2.	disagree	6.	shrink	10.	squeeze	14.	walk
3.	discuss	7.	splash	11.	squirt		
4.	enjoy	8.	split	12.	talk		

Fill in the Blanks * Llene el Espacio (page 107)

1. talks
2. enjoys
3. squeezes
4. discusses
5. split
6. squirt
7. disagrees
8. sprays
9. walks
10. build
11. entertain
12. shrink
13. splash
14. throws

Comprehension * Comprensión (page 109)

1. The Amazon River is located in South America.
2. A watershed is a region draining into a body of water.
3. The largest tropical rainforest is located in the Amazon watershed.
4. The Boto dolphins live in the Amazon River.
5. The major threats to the dolphins are pollution, deforestation, entanglement in fishing nets, and competition for fish with humans.
6. Piranhas and Anacondas live in the Amazon River.
7. The Amazon enters into the Atlantic Ocean.
8. The Amazon begins in Peru.
9. A tributary is a stream or river flowing into a larger stream or river.
10. Settlers clearing the land for farming and lumber companies harvesting trees for lumber are two things destroying the Amazon Rainforest.

Vocabulary * Vocabulario (page 110)

1.	livestock	8.	tributary
2.	culture	9.	school
3.	entanglement	10.	watershed
4.	preserve	11.	tropical
5.	nostrils	12.	dolphin
6.	rainforest	13.	native
7.	vulnerable	14.	carnivorous

Compound Sentences * Oraciones compuestas (page 111)

1. The children ate breakfast <u>and</u> then they did their chores.
2. I will fold the clothes <u>but</u> I will not put them away.
3. You may go to your friend's house <u>or</u> your friend can come here.
4. Mom will sew the pants <u>and</u> Jan will iron the skirts.
5. Dad will wash the walls <u>but</u> he will not mop the floor.
6. Mom can cook the fish <u>or</u> Dad can grill the steaks.
7. Cats like to sleep <u>and</u> kittens like to play.

8. – 12. *Answers will vary. Here are some examples.*

8. *Dad will mow the lawn and Mom will water the flowers.*
9. *Mary will clear the table and Lucy will wash the dishes.*
10. *Tom will ride his bike or he will go for a walk.*
11. *Sue can wash the car but she cannot wash the windows.*
12. *I will read a book or I will go for a hike.*

112

Lesson 17 * Lección 17

Vocabulary * Vocabulario

Describing Words 3 * Palabras de descripción 3

Coloque las palabras de vocabulario en inglés en orden alfabético. Para hacerlo, escriba primero las palabras que comienzan con <u>a</u>, luego las que comienzan con <u>b</u>, después <u>c</u>, <u>d</u>, <u>e</u>, y así sucesivamente. Si dos palabras comienzan con la misma letra, entonces considere la siguiente letra y escriba la palabra que tenga la segunda letra más cercana al principio del alfabeto.

English	Spanish	Alphabetize
1. homeless	sin hogar	1.
2. restless	impaciente	2.
3. darkness	oscuridad	3.
4. wooden	de madera	4.
5. rusty	oxidado	5.
6. rough	áspero	6.
7. tough	resistente	7.
8. thinner	más delgado	8.
9. biggest	el más grande	9.
10. famous	famoso	10.
11. enormous	enorme	11.
12. dangerous	peligroso	12.
13. nervous	nervioso	13.
14. tiny	minúsculo	14.

Fill in the Blanks * Llene el Espacio

Llene cada espacio con una palabra de la página de vocabulario. Use la palabra en español que se encuentra al final de la oración como ayuda.

1. The girl stepped on a _____ nail. | **oxidado**

2. The boy feels _____ about singing on stage. | **nervioso**

3. The white dog is _____ than the black one. | **más delgado**

4. Please place the _____ chairs around the table. | **de madera**

5. My friend blew an _____ bubble with his gum. | **enorme**

6. This meat is too _____ to eat. | **resistente**

7. The _____ person sleeps under the bridge. | **sin hogar**

8. The _____ turtle is on the large gray rock. | **el más grande**

9. Sandpaper is _____ . | **áspero**

10. It is _____ to ride a motorcycle without a helmet. | **peligroso**

11. The boys get _____ when they can't go outside. | **impaciente**

12. Your purse is too _____ to carry much. | **minúsculo**

13. That _____ person does not have much money. | **famoso**

14. The power failure left us in _____ for six hours. | **oscuridad**

114

Antarctica

Antarctica is one of the seven continents. It is the third smallest continent with only Europe and Australia being smaller. Antarctica is about 1½ times larger than the United States of America. It is the southern most continent and includes the South Pole. The South Pole is the southernmost point on the surface of the Earth. On the opposite side of the Earth is the North Pole.

Ninety-eight percent of Antarctica is covered with ice. The remaining two percent of the land is barren rock. There is little precipitation on Antarctica except at the coasts. The South Pole receives almost no rain. Antarctica is the coldest place on Earth. Temperatures reach a minimum of between -85 °C and -89 °C (-121 °F and -130 °F) in the winter and about 0 °C (32 °F) in the summer months. Antarctica has the highest average elevation of all the continents. This is one reason why Antarctica is colder than the Arctic. Much of Antarctica is more than 3 kilometers above sea level. Temperatures decrease with elevation.

As the only uninhabited continent, Antarctica has no government and belongs to no country. It is regulated by the Antarctica Treaty System. This treaty has been signed by forty-five countries. Antarctica has no permanent residents, but a number of governments maintain research stations on the continent. The number of people conducting and supporting scientific research and other work on the continent and its nearby islands varies from approximately 4000 in summer to 1000 in winter. The Antarctic Treaty System prohibits any military activity on the continent.

Antarctic sea life includes penguins, blue whales, and fur seals. Conservation acts have put regulations on fisheries but illegal fishing still remains a serious problem for the Antarctic sea animals. Commercial fishing is taking away the food for the penguins, whales and seals.

Antarctica is a cold continent but tourists visit the continent with most coming on commercial ships. The number of tourists is predicted to increase to over 80,000 by 2010. In the future, there may be stricter regulations for ships and tourism quotas because of environmental concerns caused by the influx of visitors. If you do go to Antarctica, make sure you wear sunscreen; otherwise, you may get a bad sunburn because the snow surface can reflect over 90% of the sunlight falling on it.

Comprehension Questions

Use la información en *Antarctica* para contestar las siguientes preguntas. Conteste cada pregunta con una oración completa.

1. Where is Antarctica located?

   _____

2. Write a sentence about the size of Antarctica.

   _____

3. Where is the South Pole located?

   _____

4. What covers most of Antarctica?

   _____

5. Name one reason why Antarctica is colder than the Arctic.

   _____

6. Who lives on Antarctica?

   _____

7. What kind of work is done at the research centers?

   _____

8. What governs Antarctica?

   _____

9. What is endangering the sea life at Antarctica?

   _____

10. How many letters are in the word Antarctica? Which two letters each have two in the word?

    _____

Descriptive Sentences * Oraciones descriptivas

Llene la tabla con adjetivos y verbos. Los adjetivos son palabras que describen. Los sustantivos son personas, lugares, cosas o creaturas. Los verbos son palabras de acción. La primera ya está hecha.

Article	Adjective	Adjective	Noun	Verb
The	alert	triangular	ears	listen for danger
			crutches	
A			shirt	
			women	
The			people	
A			squirrel	
The			blanket	
The			wind	
An			artist	

Ahora escriba las oraciones con la información de la tabla. La primera ya está hecha.

1. *The alert triangular ears listen for danger.*

2. _____

3. _____

4. _____

5. _____

6. _____

7. _____

8. _____

9. _____

Complex Sentences * Oraciones Complejas

Una oración compleja tiene una cláusula independiente y por lo menos una cláusula dependiente unidas por una conjunción de subordinación. Una cláusula independiente tiene un sujeto y un verbo y puede sostenerse sola (oración sencilla). Una cláusula dependiente tiene un sujeto y un verbo, pero no puede sostenerse sola (no es una oración sencilla). Las siguientes palabras son conjunciones de subordinación: *as, after, because, before, if, when* y *while*. Lea las siguientes oraciones complejas y subraye la conjunción en cada oración.

1. **As the woman brushed her teeth, she stood on one leg.**

2. **After we eat supper, we can play a game.**

3. **María is studying because she has a test tomorrow.**

4. **Before you go to school, you need to make your bed.**

5. **When José turned in his homework, he forgot to write his name on it.**

6. **While you were sleeping, the dog ran away.**

Ahora escriba sus propias oraciones complejas. Use cada una de las siguientes conjunciones: *as, after, because, before, when* y *while*. Asegúrese de que cada oración tenga una cláusula independiente y una cláusula dependiente.

7. _____

8. _____

9. _____

10. _____

11. _____

12. _____

118

Answer Key * Las Respuestas

Alphabetizing * Colocar en orden alfabético (page 113)

1.	biggest	5.	famous	9.	rough	13.	tough
2.	dangerous	6.	homeless	10.	rusty	14.	wooden
3.	darkness	7.	nervous	11.	thinner		
4.	enormous	8.	restless	12.	tiny		

Fill in the Blanks * Llene el Espacio (page 114)

1. rusty
2. nervous
3. thinner
4. wooden
5. enormous
6. tough
7. homeless
8. biggest
9. rough
10. dangerous
11. restless
12. tiny
13. famous
14. darkness

Comprehension * Comprensión (page 116)

1. Antarctica is located at the southern end of Earth.
2. Antarctica is about 11/2 times larger than the United States of America.
3. The South Pole is the southern most point on the surface of the Earth.
4. Ice covers most of Antarctica.
5. Much of Antarctica is more than 3 kilometers above sea level. Temperatures decrease with elevation.
6. Researchers live on Antarctica.
7. Scientific work is done at the research centers.
8. The Antarctic Treaty Systems governs Antarctica.
9. Illegal fishing is endangering the sea life.
10. There are ten letters in Antarctica. The letters <u>t</u> and <u>c</u> each have two in the word Antarctica.

Descriptive Sentences * Oraciones descriptivas (page 117)
Answers will vary. Here are some examples.

Article	Adjective	Adjective	Noun	Verb
The	alert	triangular	ears	listen for danger
The	tall	yellow	crutches	are used for walking
A	torn	gray	shirt	hangs on the line
The	young	lively	women	sang a song
The	tired	hungry	people	waited in line
A	frisky	brown	squirrel	ran up the tree
The	soft	blue	blanket	dried in the sun
The	cold	gusty	wind	blew the leaves
An	extremely	talented	artist	painted the picture

1. The alert triangular ears listen for danger.
2. The tall yellow crutches are used for walking.
3. A torn gray shirt hangs on the line.
4. The young lively women sang a song.
5. The tired hungry people waited in line.
6. A frisky brown squirrel ran up the tree.
7. The soft blue blanket dried in the sun.
8. The cold gusty wind blew the leaves.
9. An extremely talented artist painted the picture.

Complex Sentences * Oraciones Complejas (page 118)

1. <u>As</u> the woman brushed her teeth, she stood on one leg.
2. <u>After</u> we eat supper, we can play a game.
3. She did well on the test <u>because</u> she studied.
4. <u>Before</u> you go to school, you need to make your bed.
5. We will go to the show <u>when</u> they arrive.
6. <u>While</u> you were sleeping, the dog ran away.

7. – 12. *Answers will vary.* Here are some examples.

7. As we walked to the store, it started to rain.
8. After she did her homework, Ana called her friend.
9. The game stopped because it began to rain.
10. Before you go to school, you should eat breakfast.
11. We will eat dinner when she arrives.
12. While we were at the mall, it began to snow.

Lesson 18 * Lección 18

Vocabulary * Vocabulario

Health * Salud

Inglés	Español
1. crutches	muletas
2. stitches	puntadas
3. blind	ciego
4. lotion	loción
5. nurse	enfermera
6. bandage	vendaje
7. splinter	astilla
8. infection	infección
9. cough	tos
10. illness	enfermedad
11. hurt	dolor
12. ointment	ungüento
13. bruise	moretón
14. fever	fiebre

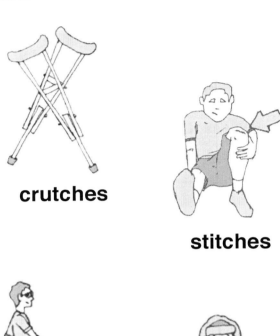

crutches

stitches

blind

lotion

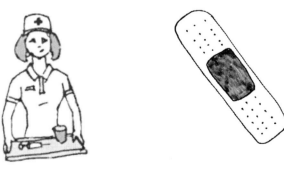

nurse

bandage

Fill in the Blanks * Llene el Espacio

Llene cada espacio con una palabra de la página de vocabulario. Use cada palabra solamente una vez. Algunas oraciones tienen dibujos al final para ayudarle. Lea la oración con cuidado porque puede necesitar añadir una s o las letras es a la palabra del vocabulario.

1. We saw many _____ at the hospital.

2. The girl _____ her knee when she slipped on the ice.

3. She puts _____ on her dry hands every morning.

4. My uncle caught an _____ when he went overseas.

5. He will use a tweezers to take out the _____ .

6. Here are some _____ to help you walk.

7. Her son has had several _____ this past year.

8. My sister has a big purple _____ on her knee.

9. Mom put twelve _____ in the first aid kit.

10. You can not go to school if you have a _____ .

11. The _____ woman has a white cane with a red tip.

12. Clean your cut with soap and water then rub on this _____ before putting on the bandage.

13. Pam had to get eight _____ on her elbow.

14. Please cover your mouth when you _____ .

Oprah Winfrey

Almost everyone has heard of Oprah Winfrey. She has been the host of the Oprah Winfrey Show since 1986. She is also a magazine publisher, has been an actress, has been ranked the richest African American of the 20th century, and many believe she is the most influential woman in the world. Do you know that she is also a very philanthropic person?

At the age of 52, Oprah said she started her most important work yet. She opened the Oprah Winfrey Leadership Academy, an innovative high school, just outside the city of Johannesburg, South Africa. The school is for impoverished girls and the charter classes started with girls ranging in age from eleven to thirteen. The goal of the school is to teach and inspire young South African girls to become leaders in their communities. Oprah says her own success came from a strong background in reading and learning, and that the greatest gift you can give is the gift of learning.

Many of the 75 girls who were selected for the school came from homes with no water or electricity; and had to sleep on dirt floors. Many have lost a parent to AIDS and others have been abandoned. Before being interviewed by Oprah, the girls were chosen from teachers across South Africa for academic excellence and early displays of leadership

In 2002, when she announced her plans to build this school, she donated $10 million. Since then, her donation has grown to more than $40 million. Besides being a great institution for learning, the school is also a beautiful home for girls. The buildings have artwork by artists from all over South Africa and every classroom has an outdoor teaching space and sometimes a garden. Each classroom has only fifteen girls. Besides classrooms and dormitories, the campus also includes a library with plush seating around a fireplace, a cafeteria, a gym, a magnificent amphitheater, and state-of-the-art technology.

Oprah plans to continue her most important work by building academies in other countries for gifted impoverished children. You go girl!

Comprehension Questions

Use la información en *Oprah Winfrey* para contestar las siguientes preguntas. Conteste cada pregunta con una oración completa.

1. Write a sentence describing Oprah Winfrey.

   _____

2. What does philanthropic mean?

   _____

3. At what age did Oprah start her most important work?

   _____

4. What is her "most important work"?

   _____

5. Describe the students who come to the academy.

   _____

6. How many girls were in the charter class?

   _____

7. What does charter mean in this story?

   _____

8. Name some of the buildings found on the campus.

   _____

9. Where is the school located?

   _____

10. Why did Oprah start this academy?

   _____

Sentence Practice * Práctica de oraciones

Lea las siguientes oraciones. En cada oración, subraye el sujeto una vez, encierre la palabra de acción en un cuadro, dibuje un círculo alrededor del adjetivo y ponga una x encima del artículo (si hay un artículo). Un adjetivo describe un sustantivo. El sujeto es un sustantivo. Los tres artículos son *a*, *an* y *the.* Recuerde encontrar la palabra de acción primero y luego el sujeto que está realizando la acción. La primera ya está hecha.

1. The (cold) <u>wind</u> blew.

2. A big bubble floated.

3. The tall woman shops.

4. Four bees buzz.

5. An old dog walks.

Vuelva a escribir las cinco oraciones anteriores añadiendo la información sobre dónde a cada oración.

6. _____

7. _____

8. _____

9. _____

10. _____

Ahora escriba cinco oraciones suyas asegurándose de que cada una tenga un adjetivo que describa el sujeto, un verbo e información sobre dónde. Su oración también puede incluir un artículo.

11. _____

12. _____

13. _____

14. _____

15. _____

Sentence Practice * Práctica de oraciones

Lea las siguientes oraciones. Cada una tiene una cláusula con *when*. Subraye la cláusula con *when* en cada oración. La primera ya está hecha.

1. <u>When the wind blew</u>, the kite flew up high.

2. When it began to drizzle, we ran for cover.

3. We will go home when my dad arrives.

4. When the weather gets nice, we will have a picnic.

5. Put on your jacket when it gets cold.

6. When it stops raining, you can go out and play.

7. When you arrive, please give me a call.

8. When the bell rang, the children ran to school.

Ahora escriba sus propias oraciones. Asegúrese de que cada una tenga una cláusula con *when*.

9. _____

10. _____

11. _____

12. _____

13. _____

14. _____

15. _____

16. _____

Answer Key * Las Respuestas

Fill in the Blanks * Llene el Espacio (page 121)

1. nurses
2. hurt
3. lotion
4. infection
5. splinter
6. crutches
7. illnesses
8. bruise
9. bandages
10. fever
11. blind
12. ointment
13. stitches
14. cough

Comprehension * Comprensión (page 123)

1. Oprah Winfrey is the host of the Oprah Winfrey Show.
2. Philanthropic means being charitable towards others.
3. Oprah Winfrey was 52 years old when she started her most important work.
4. Her most important work is a school she established for girls in South Africa.
5. The students are intelligent young girls from impoverished backgrounds.
6. There were 75 girls in the charter class.
7. In the story, charter means the first class.
8. Some of the buildings on campus are dormitories, library, cafeteria, and a gym.
9. The school is located in Johannesburg, South Africa.
10. She started the school because she believes the greatest gift you can give is the gift of learning.

Sentence Practice * Práctica de oraciones (page 124)

	Article	Adjective	Subject	Action Word
1.	The	cold	wind	blew
2.	A	big	bubble	floated
3.	The	tall	woman	shops
4.		Four	bees	buzz
5.	An	old	dog	walks

6. - 10. *Answers will vary. Here are some examples.*
6. The cold wind blew outside.
7. The big bubble floated in the air.
8. The tall woman shops at the mall.
9. Four bees buzz in the garden.
10. An old dog walks down the street.

11. – 15. *Answers will vary. Here are some examples.*
11. The brown squirrel ran up the tree.
12. The spotted dog dashed across the street.
13. The little mouse scurried under the chair.
14. The tall girl skipped around the yard.
15. The chubby baby sleeps in his cradle.

Sentence Practice * Práctica de oraciones (page 125)

1. <u>When the wind blew</u>, the kite flew up high.
2. <u>When it began to drizzle</u>, we ran for cover.
3. We will go home <u>when my dad arrives</u>.
4. <u>When the weather gets nice</u>, we will have a picnoc.
5. Put on your jacket <u>when it gets cold</u>.
6. <u>When it stops raining</u>, you can go out and play.
7. <u>When you arrive</u>, please give me a call.
8. <u>When the bell rang</u>, the children ran to school.

9. – 16. *Answers will vary. Here are some examples.*
9. When I am older, I will go to school.
10. Put on your hat when you go outside.
11. When it rains, our roof leaks.
12. When I go to the party, I will bring a gift.
13. When I go to the store, I will buy a book.
14. When you drive the car, don't go too fast.
15. I like to walk on the beach when the weather is warm.
16. I like to eat popcorn when I watch a movie.

Lesson 19 * Lección 19

Vocabulary * Vocabulario

School * Escuela

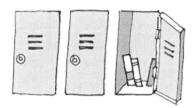

lockers
armarios

exam
examen

erase
borrar

teacher
maestra

read
leer

team
equipo

desk
escritorio

student
estudiante

paper
papel

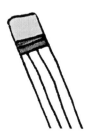

eraser
borrador

pencil
lápiz

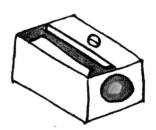

sharpener
sacapuntas

Fill in the Blanks * Llene el Espacio

Llene cada espacio con una palabra de la página de vocabulario. Use la figura al final de la oración para ayudarse. Lea la oración con cuidado porque puede necesitar añadir una <u>s</u> o las letras <u>es</u> a la palabra del vocabulario.

1. **Here is a new electric pencil _____ for our class.**

2. **My brother is the pitcher for the school's baseball _____.**

3. **You need to completely _____ your mistake.**

4. **Kim has three _____ in her purse.**

5. **The _____ will give the final exam on Friday.**

6. **These _____ have the company's name on them.**

7. **Tim _____ when he gets home from work.**

8. **The _____ gave their teacher a present.**

9. **The teacher put the _____ in rows.**

10. **They will paint the _____ on Thursday.**

11. **Here is _____ for your subtraction problems.**

12. **He did poorly on two of his _____ .**

Global Warming

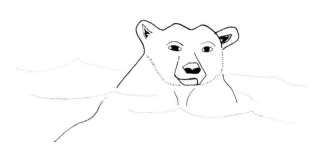

Do you believe in global warming? Some people do and others do not. I believe in global warming. Here are my reasons why.

First of all, what is global warming? Global warming is the increase in the average temperature of the Earth's atmosphere and oceans in recent decades and its predicted continuation into the future. Earth has warmed by about 1°F over the past 100 years. What causes global warming? Global warming is caused by increasing the amount of greenhouse gases in the atmosphere. What are greenhouse gases? Greenhouse gases are any gas that absorbs infra-red radiation in the atmosphere. For example, carbon dioxide is a greenhouse gas. Having just the right amount of greenhouse gas is good because it keeps our earth the right temperature for people. But when there are too much greenhouse gases then there is too much radiated heat and the earth warms up. What causes the increase in greenhouse gases? Deforestation causes an increase in greenhouse gases. Trees, like most living things, are made mostly of carbon. When forests are cut and burned the carbon in trees is turned into a gas called carbon dioxide which is one of the most important greenhouse gases. People also increase the amount of carbon dioxide in the air by burning fossil fuels. Fossil fuels are fuels that are formed in the Earth from plant or animal remains such as coal, oil and natural gas. Oil is used to make gasoline; and coal and natural gas are used in power plants to produce electricity. Even global temperature increase of less than one degree can cause problems such as sea levels rising and changes in rainfall. Carbon dioxide is the most common greenhouse gas emitted from human activities.

What can people do to stop global warming? They can drive smaller cars, carpool, ride a bike, use public transportation or walk. Turn off lights, televisions, and computers when you're not using them. Plant trees. Trees absorb carbon dioxide. Recycle and use products made from recycled materials. Buy products with the ENERGY STAR® label because these products are made to save energy.

One animal that has become vulnerable with the warming climate is the polar bear. As the climate gets warmer, the ice is melting where polar bears live. Bears use the ice environment to find food, reproduce and survive. With the ice melting, some female bears fail to gain enough weight during the summer to be able to breed. Others are drowning as they must swim farther and farther to find ice. Some hungry bears are raiding village dumps and are sometimes shot. On land, polar bears are clumsy hunters so their existence is threatened as the Arctic keeps melting.

Stop global warming! Use less fossil fuels.

Comprehension Questions

Use la información en *Global Warming* para contestar las siguientes preguntas. Conteste cada pregunta con una oración completa.

1. What is global warming?

    _____

2. What is the greenhouse effect?

    _____

3. What are fossil fuels?

    _____

4. What causes an increase in greenhouse gases?

    _____

5. What is the most common greenhouse gas emitted by human activities?

    _____

6. Even a global temperature increase of less than one degree can cause what kind of problems?

    _____

7. Name three things people can do to stop global warming.

    _____

8. What is one animal that has become vulnerable with global warming?

    _____

9. Why has it become vulnerable?

    _____

10. Do you believe in global warming? Why? Or Why not?

Sentence Practice * Práctica de oraciones

Lea las siguientes oraciones. En cada oración subraye el sujeto una vez, encierre en un cuadro la palabra de acción (verbo), dibuje un círculo alrededor del adverbio y ponga una x encima del artículo (si hay un artículo). En estas oraciones, el adverbio modifica al verbo diciendo *cómo*, *cuándo* o *dónde*. Los tres artículos son *a*, *an* y *the*. Recuerde encontrar la palabra de acción primero y después el sujeto que realize la acción. La primera ya está hecha.

1. The <u>rabbit</u> runs quickly

2. A turtle crawls slowly.

3. The girl does her job gladly.

4. Two girls works quietly.

5. An otter swims gracefully.

Vuelva a escribir las cinco oraciones anteriores añadiendo información sobre *dónde* o una cláusula con *when* a cada oración.

6. _____

7. _____

8. _____

9. _____

10. _____

Ahora escriba cinco oraciones suyas asegurándose de que cada una tenga un sujeto, un verbo y un adverbio que modifique al verbo. Su oración también puede incluir un artículo.

11. _____

12. _____

13. _____

14. _____

15. _____

Sentence Practice * Práctica de oraciones

En esta página, cada oración necesita un sujeto, una parte de acción y una cláusula con *when*. Lea cada oración y después decida cuál parte falta. Si falta el sujeto, escriba una S al final de la oración. Si falta la parte de acción, escirba V (por verbo). Si falta la cláusula con *when*, escriba una W. Después escriba una palabra o unas palabras para la parte que falta. La primera ya está hecha.

1. When the bell rings, the ___*children*___ may leave. __S__

2. When we eat breakfast, dad _____ the newspaper. _____

3. When the wind blows, _____ fly down the street. _____

4. _____ , the children jump in puddles. _____

5. The children are careful _____ . _____

6. When he opened the window, a _____ flew in. _____

7. He goes fishing _____ . _____

8. When the sun sets, the _____ gets colder. _____

9. _____ , the dog gets restless. _____

10. _____ , the boy scraped his leg. _____

11. When he laughs, his _____ hurts. _____

12. When it rains, the _____ sleeps under the bridge. _____

13. _____ will go when the children are ready. _____

14. When the train arrived, _____ jumped on. _____

15. Tom _____ to bed when he gets sleepy. _____

16. My uncles _____ when the weather gets cold. _____

17. When we are on vacation, my dad _____ . _____

132

Answer Key * Las Respuestas

Fill in the Blanks * Llene el Espacio (page 128)

1. sharpener
2. team
3. erase
4. erasers
5. teacher
6. pencils
7. reads
8. students
9. desks
10. lockers
11. paper
12. exams

Comprehension * Comprensión (page 130)

1. Global warming is the increase in the average temperature of the Earth's atmosphere and oceans in recent decades.
2. Greenhouse gases are any gas that absorbs infra-red radiation in the atmosphere.
3. Fossil fuels are fuels that are formed in the Earth from plant or animal remains.
4. Deforestation causes an increase in greenhouse gases.
5. Carbon dioxide is the most common greenhouse gas emitted by human activities.
6. An increase of less than one degree can cause the sea levels to rise and changes in rainfall.
7. People can drive smaller cars, carpool, ride a bike, walk, or use public transportation.
8. The polar bear has become vulnerable with global warming.
9. They have become vulnerable because the ice is melting where the polar bears live.
10. I believe in global warming because the scientific facts support the existence of global warming.

Sentence Practice * Práctica de oraciones (page 131)

	Article	Subject	Verb	Adverb
1.	The	rabbit	runs	quickly
2.	A	turtle	crawls	slowly
3.	The	girl	does	gladly
4.		girls	work	quietly
5.	An	otter	swims	gracefully

6. - 10. *Answers will vary. Here are some examples.*
6. The rabbit runs quickly when chased by the dog.
7. The turtle crawls slowly towards the rock.
8. When the task is fun, the girl does her job gladly.
9. Two girls work quietly in the library.
10. An otter swims gracefully in the ocean.

11. – 15. *Answers will vary. Here are some examples.*
11. *The boy speaks slowly.*
12. *The bird flies high.*
13. *The engine revs loudly.*
14. *The thunder rumbles softly.*
15. *The lady sings happily.*

Sentence Practice * Práctica de oraciones (page 132)
Answers will vary except for the parts of speech. Here are some examples.

	Subject (S)	Verb (V)	When Clause (W)
1.	children		
2.		reads	
3.	leaves		
4.			
5.			When it rains
6.	moth		when they play
7.			
8.	air		when the sun goes down
9.			
10.			When it thunders
11.	side		When he fell
12.	man		
13.	We		
14.	Bill		
15.		goes	
16.		ski	
17.		hikes	

Lesson 20 * Lección 20

Vocabulary * Vocabulario

Verbs 4 * Verbos 4

Coloque las palabras de vocabulario en inglés en orden alfabético. Para hacerlo, escriba primero las palabras que comienzan con <u>a</u>, luego las que comienzan con <u>b</u>, después <u>c</u>, <u>d</u>, <u>e</u>, y así sucesivamente. Si dos palabras comienzan con la misma letra, entonces considere la siguiente letra y escriba la palabra que tenga la segunda letra más cercana al principio del alfabeto.

English	Spanish	Alphabetize
1. hopping	saltando	1.
2. shopping	comprando	2.
3. dripping	goteando	3.
4. tapped	tamborilear	4.
5. propose	proponer	5.
6. earn	ganar	6.
7. heard	escuchó	7.
8. learn	aprender	8.
9. told	dijo	9.
10. work	trabajar	10.
11. sew	coser	11.
12. turn	voltear	12.
13. surf	hacer surf	13.
14. sold	vendió	14.

Fill in the Blanks * Llene el Espacio

Llene cada espacio con una palabra de la página de vocabulario. Use la palabra en español que se encuentra al final de la oración como ayuda. Lea la oración con cuidado porque puede necesitar añadir una <u>s</u> o las letras <u>es</u> a la palabra del vocabulario.

1. Tom _____ twenty dollars an hour at his job. | **ganar**

2. Pam _____ every morning before school. | **hace surf**

3. Al _____ his fingers on the table. | **tamborilear**

4. My dad _____ in the hotel's kitchen. | **trabajar**

5. We _____ the news on the radio. | **escuchó**

6. We were _____ wet after being caught in the rain. | **goteando**

7. You need to _____ at the next corner. | **voltear**

8. The children are _____ on the pavement. | **saltando**

9. My mother _____ clothes for a living. | **coser**

10. You will ____ many things when you go to college. | **aprender**

11. He will _____ to his girl friend on Saturday night. | **proponer**

12. Let's go _____ this weekend. | **comprando**

13. We _____ our car on the internet. | **vendió**

14. She _____ her mother about the accident. | **dijo**

The Arctic

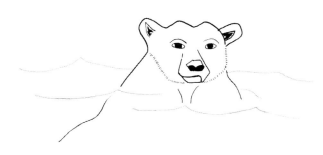

The Arctic is not a continent or a country. Instead it includes the northern parts of Canada, Greenland, Russia, United States, Iceland, Norway, Sweden, and Finland as well as the Arctic Ocean. The Arctic is the area north of the Arctic Circle. The Arctic Circle is one of the five major circles of latitude on maps of the Earth. The Arctic is mostly an ice-covered ocean surrounded by treeless, frozen ground. There is much life at the Arctic including fish and marine mammals, birds, land animals and people.

The people at the Arctic have adapted to its cold and extreme conditions. The primary residents of the Arctic include the Eskimos (Inuits), Saami, and Russians, with an overall population exceeding 2 million. The indigenous Eskimos have lived in the area for over 9,000 years, and many have now given up much of their traditional hunting and fishing to work in the oil fields and the varied support villages.

In the mid winter months, the sun never rises and temperatures can be as low as -50° F. In the summer months, there are 24 hours of sunlight which melts the seas and topsoil, and is the main cause of icebergs breaking off from the frozen north and floating south.

The Arctic land is mainly tundra. This flat frozen ground is treeless and is covered with plants like moss and lichen, which caribou like to eat. The caribou is a member of the deer family. Another Arctic animal is the wolverine which is not related to the wolf but instead to the weasel. The white Arctic fox camouflages well into the snowy environment. The polar bear is probably the most popular Arctic animal. They spend most of their time on ice floes. They are the largest land meat-eater in the world and the largest of the bear family.

Average temperatures in the Arctic region are rising twice as fast as they are elsewhere in the world. Arctic ice is getting thinner, melting and breaking apart. Ice that has been around for over 3,000 years is starting to crack and break into pieces. Along Arctic coastlines, entire villages may need to move because they're in danger of being swamped. Many native people of the Arctic view global warming as a threat to their way of life.

The Arctic is made up of eight different countries along with the Arctic Ocean. Many animals and people make their home in the Arctic.

Comprehension Questions

Use la información en *The Arctic* para contestar las siguientes preguntas. Conteste cada pregunta con una oración completa.

1. Where is the Arctic located?

   _____

2. How many countries are part of the Arctic?

   _____

3. Write one sentence to describe the Arctic.

   _____

4. Who are the primary residents of the Arctic?

   _____

5. How do many Eskimos make their living?

   _____

6. How cold can it get at the Arctic in the winter?

   _____

7. Write one sentence to describe the Arctic summer.

   _____

8. Name three animals that live in Arctic?

   _____

9. Why are many native people of the Arctic concerned about global warming?

   _____

10. What is the third letter in the word Arctic?

   _____

Verbs * Verbos

Use las palabras del cuadro para escribir el verbo correcto debajo de cada dibujo.

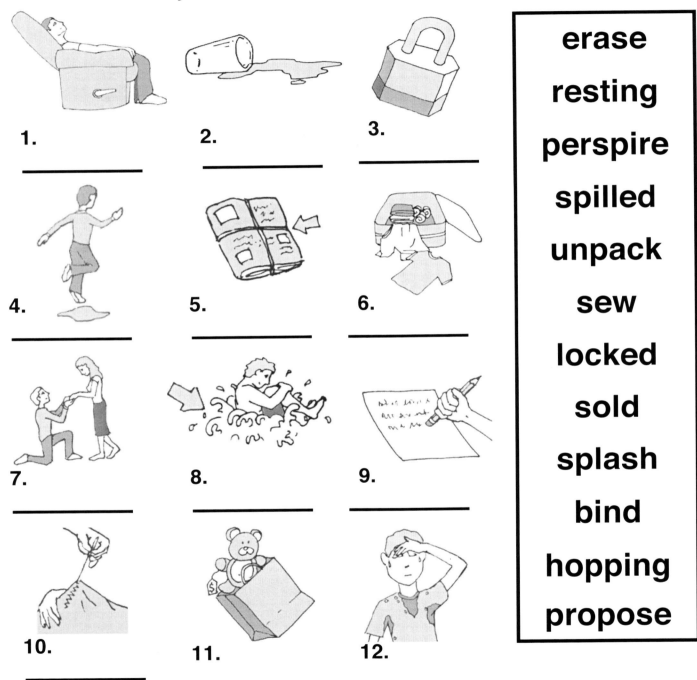

1. _____

2. _____

3. _____

4. _____

5. _____

6. _____

7. _____

8. _____

9. _____

10. _____

11. _____

12. _____

erase

resting

perspire

spilled

unpack

sew

locked

sold

splash

bind

hopping

propose

En otra hoja escriba una oración con cada palabra.

Categories * Categorías

Escriba el nombre de cada figura en la categoría correcta.

Animals	People	Places	Things

Answer Key * Las Respuestas

Alphabetizing * Colocar en orden alfabético (page 134)

1.	dripping	5.	learn	9.	sold	13.	turn
2.	earn	6.	propose	10.	surf	14.	work
3.	heard	7.	sew	11.	tapped		
4.	hopping	8.	shopping	12.	told		

Fill in the Blanks * Llene el Espacio (page 135)

1. earns
2. surfs
3. tapped
4. works
5. heard
6. dripping
7. turn
8. hopping
9. sews
10. learn
11. propose
12. shopping
13. sold
14. told

Comprehension * Comprensión (page 137)

1. The Arctic is the area north of the Arctic Circle.
2. Eight countries are part of the Arctic.
3. The Arctic is mostly an ice covered ocean surrounded by treeless, frozen ground.
4. The primary residents of the arctic are Eskimos, Saami, and Russians.
5. Many Eskimos make their living working in the oil fields.
6. In the winter, the temperature can be as low as -50 F.
7. In the summer, there are 24 hours of sunlight.
8. Caribou, the white Arctic fox, and polar bears live in the Arctic.
9. Many native people of the Arctic view global warming as a threat to their way of life.
10. The third letter in the work Arctic is 'c'.

Verbs * Verbos (page 138)

1. resting
2. spilled
3. locked
4. hopping
5. bind
6. unpack
7. propose
8. splash
9. erase
10. sew
11. sold
12. perspire

Categories * Categorías (page 139)

Animals	People	Places	Things
bird	boys	party	dresses
shrimp	girl	apartment	table
squirrel	nurse	Earth	boxes
bull	women	kitchen	feather

English Translation of Spanish Directions

Lesson 1

Page 2: Fill in each blank with a word from the vocabulary page. Use the picture at the end of the sentence to help you. Read the sentence carefully because you may need to add <u>s</u> or <u>es</u> to the vocabulary word.

Page 4: Use the information in *Sea Turtles* to answer the following questions. Answer each question in a complete sentence.

Page 5: A prefix is a group of letters added to the beginning of a word to change its meaning. On this page we will use the following prefixes: <u>in</u>, <u>re</u>, <u>un</u>. The prefixes <u>in</u> and <u>un</u> mean *not*. The prefix <u>re</u> means *again*. **Write** the meaning of each of the following words. The first one has been done for you. **Complete** each sentence with a word from above.

Page 6: Homophones are words that sound alike, but are spelled differently and have different meanings. **Above** each sentence are two homophones. Chose the correct one for each sentence.

Lesson 2

Page 9: Fill in each blank with a word from the vocabulary page. Use the picture at the end of the sentence to help you. Read the sentence carefully because you may need to add <u>s</u> or <u>es</u> to the vocabulary word.

Page 11: Use the information in *Archie Carr* to answer the following questions. Answer each question in a complete sentence.

Page 12: A prefix is a group of letters added to the beginning of a word to change its meaning. On this page we will use the following prefixes: <u>dis</u>, <u>im</u>, <u>non</u>. The prefixes <u>dis</u> and <u>im</u> mean *opposite*. The prefix <u>non</u> means *not, no,* or *without*. **Write** the meaning of each of the following words. The first one has been done for you. **Complete** each sentence with a word from above.

Page 13: Many words have several popular meanings. Write two sentences for each word making sure each sentence uses a different meaning of the word.

Lesson 3

Page 16: Fill in each blank with a word from the vocabulary page. Use the picture at the end of the sentence to help you. Read the sentence carefully because you may need to add <u>s</u> or <u>es</u> to the vocabulary word.

Page 18: Use the information in *Channel Islands National Park* to answer the following questions. Answer each question in a complete sentence.

Page 19: A prefix is a group of letters added to the beginning of a word to change its meaning. On this page we will use the following prefixes: <u>mis-</u>, <u>pre-</u>, <u>under-</u>. The prefix <u>mis-</u> means *wrongly*. The prefix <u>pre-</u> means *before*. The prefix <u>under-</u> means *below* or *less than*. **Write** the meaning of each of the following words. The first one has been done for you. **Complete** each sentence with a word from above.

Page 20: Next to each word, write the word that means the opposite or almost the opposite. Use the words in the box for your answers.

Lesson 4

Page 23: Fill in each blank with a word from the vocabulary page. Use the picture at the end of the sentence to help you. Read the sentence carefully because you may need to add <u>s</u> or <u>es</u> to the vocabulary word.

Page 25: Use the information in *Mountain Biking* to answer the following questions. Answer each question in a complete sentence.

Page 26: All the words for the table below can be found in the *Mountain Biking* story.

Page 27: Next to each word, write the word that means the same or almost the same. Use the words in the box for your answers.

Lesson 5

Page 29: Alphabetize the English vocabulary words. To alphabetize, write all the <u>a</u> words first, then the <u>b</u>, then <u>c</u>, <u>d</u>, <u>e</u>, and so forth. If two words begin with the same letter, then look at the next letter and write the word which has the second letter closest to the beginning of the alphabet.

Page 30: Fill in each blank with a word from the vocabulary page. Read the sentence carefully because you may need to add <u>s</u> or <u>es</u> to the vocabulary word.

Page 32: Use the information in *Camino de Santiago* to answer the following questions. Answer each question in a complete sentence.

Page 33: The suffix <u>ed</u> is added to verbs to show past tense. It can be spoken phonetically in three different ways: /ed/ as in *planted*, /d/ as in *called*, and /t/ as in *helped*. When adding a suffix to a word that ends in a silent e, drop the <u>e</u> if the suffix begins with a vowel. Do not drop the <u>e</u> if the suffix begins with a consonant. **Add** <u>ed</u> to each of the following action words (verbs). Then write which sound the ending <u>ed</u> makes. The first one has been done for you. **Complete** each sentence with a word from above that has the <u>ed suffix.</u>

Page 34: Read each pair of words. Then decide if each pair is an *antonym, synonym,* or *homophone*. The first one has been done for you.

Lesson 6

Page 37: Fill in each blank with a word from the vocabulary page. Use the picture at the end of the sentence to help you. Read the sentence carefully because you may need to add <u>s</u> or <u>es</u> to the vocabulary word.

Page 39: Use the information in *Brine Shrimp* to answer the following questions. Answer each question in a complete sentence.

Page 40: A suffix is a group of letters added to the end of a word to change its meaning. On this page we will use the following suffixes: <u>-ful</u>, <u>-less</u>, <u>-ous</u>. The suffixes <u>-ful</u> and <u>-ous</u> mean *filled with.* The suffix <u>-less</u> means *without.* **Write** the meaning of each of the following words. The first one has been done for you. **Complete** each sentence with a word from above.

Page 41: An idiom is an expression or phrase whose meaning may be unrelated to the meaning of the words in the expression or phrase. For example: "keep your eyes peeled" means *look carefully.* **Complete** each sentence with a idiom from above.

Lesson 7

Page 44: Fill in each blank with a word from the vocabulary page. Use the picture at the end of the sentence to help you. Read the sentence carefully because you may need to add <u>s</u>, <u>es</u>, or <u>ed</u> to the vocabulary word.

Page 46: Use the information in *Fashion Models* to answer the following questions. Answer each question in a complete sentence.

Page 47: Analogies are comparisons. They show relationships between words. Complete each analogy below. Use the words on the right for your answers. The first one has been done for you.

Page 48: A suffix is a group of letters added to the end of a word to change its meaning. On this page we will use the following suffixes: <u>-ly</u>, <u>-en</u>, <u>-est</u>, <u>-ness</u>. The suffix <u>-ly</u> means *how* or *to what extent*, <u>-en</u> means *make or made of*, <u>-est</u> means *most*, <u>-ness</u> means *having*. Use the words on the right for your answers.

Lesson 8

Page 51: Fill in each blank with a word from the vocabulary page. Use the picture at the end of the sentence to help you. Read the sentence carefully because you may need to add <u>s</u> or <u>es</u> to the vocabulary word.

Page 53: Use the information in *Mosquitoes* to answer the following questions. Answer each question in a complete sentence.

Page 54: A similie is a figure of speech linking two unlike things by using the words *like* or *as*. Use the words at the right to complete the following common similies. The first one has been done for you.

Page 55: Read the words at the right and then write them under the correct category.

Lesson 9

Page 58: Fill in each blank with a word from the vocabulary page. Use the picture at the end of the sentence to help you. Read the sentence carefully because you may need to add <u>s</u> or <u>es</u> to the vocabulary word.

Page 60: Use the information in *Mount Everest* to answer the following questions. Answer each question in a complete sentence.

Page 61: Analogies are comparisons. They show relationships between words. Complete each analogy below. Use the words on the right for your answers. The first one has been done for you.

Page 62: All the words for the table below can be found in the *Mount Everest* story.

Lesson 10

Page 65: Fill in each blank with a word from the vocabulary page. Use the picture at the end of the sentence to help you. Read the sentence carefully because you may need to add <u>s</u> or <u>es</u> to the vocabulary word.

Page 67: Use the information in *Bill and Melinda Gates Foundation* to answer the following questions. Answer each question in a complete sentence.

Page 68: Every sentence must have four things: a subject part, a predicate (verb) part, a punctuation mark at the end, and a capital letter to begin the sentence. Write sentences by matching the subject part with the predicate part. The first one has been done for you. Keep this page because you will be using these answers in the following lesson.

Page 69: Circle the word that relates the least to the other three.

Lesson 11

Page 72: Fill in each blank with a word from the vocabulary page. Use the picture at the end of the sentence to help you. Read the sentence carefully because you may need to add <u>s</u> or <u>es</u> to the vocabulary word.

Page 74: Use the information in *Iran* to answer the following questions. Answer each question in a complete sentence.

Page 75: Fill in the chart with adjectives and verbs. Adjectives are describing words. Nouns are person, places, things, or creatures. Verbs are action words. The first one has been done for you. **Now** write the sentences with the information from the chart. The first one has been done for you.

Page 76: Use the sentences from page 68 to do this activity. Add *where* information to each sentence. Use the suggestions in the box. The first one has been done for you. Keep this page because you will be using these answers in the following lesson.

Lesson 12

Page 78: Alphabetize the English vocabulary words. To alphabetize, write all the <u>a</u> words first, then the <u>b</u>, then <u>c</u>, <u>d</u>, <u>e</u>, and so forth. If two words begin with the same letter, then look at the next letter and write the word which has the second letter closest to the beginning of the alphabet.

Page 79: Fill in each blank with a word from the vocabulary page. Use the Spanish word at the end of the sentence to help you. Read the sentence carefully because you may need to add <u>s</u> or <u>es</u> to the vocabulary word.

Page 81: Use the information in *Continents* to answer the following questions. Answer each question in a complete sentence.

Page 82: All the words for the table below can be found in the Continents story.

Page 83: Use the sentences from page 76 to do this activity. Add a descriptive word about the subject to each sentence. Use the suggestions in the box. After you've added the adjective, add an article at the beginning of the sentences that need one. The first two have been done for you. Save this page because you will use these answers in the following lesson.

Lesson 13

Page 86: Fill in each blank with a word from the vocabulary page. Use the number at the end of the sentence to help you.

Page 88: Use the information in *The Nile River* to answer the following questions. Answer each question in a complete sentence.

Page 89: Use the sentences from page 83 to do this activity. Add *when* information to the beginning of each sentence. Use the suggestions in the box. The first one has been done for you.

Page 90: Draw a circle around the eighteen animals. **In** the chart below, write the eighteen animals under the correct animal group.

Lesson 14

Page 92: Alphabetize the English vocabulary words. To alphabetize, write all the <u>a</u> words first, then the <u>b</u>, then <u>c</u>, <u>d</u>, <u>e</u>, and so forth. If two words begin with the same letter, then look at the next letter and write the word which has the second letter closest to the beginning of the alphabet.

Page 93: Fill in each blank with a word from the vocabulary page. Use the Spanish word at the end of the sentence to help you.

Page 95: Use the information in *Iraq* to answer the following questions. Answer each question in a complete sentence.

Page 96: Read each sentence. Underline the simple subject and put a square around the simple verb. Every sentence must have a verb (an action word) and a subject (person, thing, place, or creature that does the action.) Find the action word first and then find the subject that is doing the action. The first one has been done for you.

Page 97: Write six new words by adding the prefixes and suffixes to the root word. The first one has been done for you. **Use** one of the new words in each sentence. **Add** a prefix and a suffix to the rootword to fill in the blank.

Lesson 15

Page 99: Alphabetize the English vocabulary words. To alphabetize, write all the <u>a</u> words first, then the <u>b</u>, then <u>c</u>, <u>d</u>, <u>e</u>, and so forth. If two words begin with the same letter, then look at the next letter and write the word which has the second letter closest to the beginning of the alphabet.

Page 100: Fill in each blank with a word from the vocabulary page. Use the Spanish word at the end of the sentence to help you.

Page 102: Use the information in *Amelia Earhart* to answer the following questions. Answer each question in a complete sentence.

Page 103: On this page each sentence needs a subject part, an action part, and a *where* part. Read each sentence and then decide which part is missing. If the subject part is missing write S at the end of the sentence. If the action part is missing write V (for verb). If the *where* part is missing write W. Then write in a word or words for the missing part. The first one has been done for you.

Page 104: Write six new words by adding the prefixes and suffixes to the root word. The first one has been done for you. **Use** one of the new words in each sentence. **Add** a prefix and a suffix to the rootword to fill in the blank.

Lesson 16

Page 106: Alphabetize the English vocabulary words. To alphabetize, write all the <u>a</u> words first, then the <u>b</u>, then <u>c</u>, <u>d</u>, <u>e</u>, and so forth. If two words begin with the same letter, then look at the next letter and write the word which has the second letter closest to the beginning of the alphabet.

Page 107: Fill in each blank with a word from the vocabulary page. Use the Spanish word at the end of the sentence to help you. Read the sentence carefully because you may need to add s or es to the vocabulary word.

Page 109: Use the information in *The Amazon River* to answer the following questions. Answer each question in a complete sentence.

Page 110: All the words for the table below can be found in *The Amazon River* story.

Page 111: A compound sentence has two or more independent clauses joined by a coordinating conjunction. An independent clause has a subject and a verb and can stand alone (simple sentence). The following words are coordinating conjunctions: *and, but,* and *or.* Read the following compound sentences and underline the conjunction in each sentence. **Now** write your own compound sentences. Make sure each sentence has one of the following conjunctions: *and, but, or.* Make sure each sentence has two independent clauses. Each clause must have a subject and verb and can stand alone.

Lesson 17

Page 113: Alphabetize the English vocabulary words. To alphabetize, write all the a words first, then the b, then c, d, e, and so forth. If two words begin with the same letter, then look at the next letter and write the word which has the second letter closest to the beginning of the alphabet.

Page 114: Fill in each blank with a word from the vocabulary page. Use the Spanish word at the end of the sentence to help you.

Page 116: Use the information in *Antarctica* to answer the following questions. Answer each question in a complete sentence.

Page 117: Fill in the chart with adjectives and verbs. Adjectives are describing words. Nouns are person, places, things, or creatures. Verbs are action words. The first one has been done for you. **Now** write the sentences with the information from the chart. The first one has been done for you.

Page 118: A complex sentence has one independent clause and at least one dependent clause joined by a subordinating conjunction. An independent clause has a subject and a verb and can stand alone (simple sentence). A dependent clause has a subject and verb but cannot stand alone (not a simple sentence). The following words are subordinating conjunctions: *as, after, because, before, if, when,* and *while.* Read the following complex sentences and underline the conjunction in each sentence. **Now** write your own complex sentences. Use each of the following conjunctions: *as, after, because, before, when,* and *while.* Make sure each sentence has an independent clause and a dependent clause.

Lesson 18

Page 121: Fill in each blank with a word from the vocabulary page. Use each word once. Some sentence have pictures at the end to help you. Read the sentence carefully because you may need to add s or es to the vocabulary word.

Page 123: Use the information in *Oprah Winfrey* to answer the following questions. Answer each question in a complete sentence.

Page 124: Read the following sentences. For each sentence underline the subject once, draw a square around the action word, draw a circle around the adjective, and put an x above the article (if there is an article). An adjective describes a noun. The subject is a noun. The three articles are *a, an*, and *the*. Remember to find the action word first and then the subject that is doing the action. The first one has been done for you. **Rewrite** the above five sentences adding *where* information to each sentence. **Now** write five sentences of your own making sure each has an adjective to describe the subject, a verb, and *where* information. Your sentence can also include an article.

Page 125: Read the following sentences. Each one has a *when* clause. Underline the *when* clause in each sentence. The first one has been done for you. Now write your own sentences. Make sure each one has a when clause.

Lesson 19

Page 128: Fill in each blank with a word from the vocabulary page. Use the picture at the end of the sentence to help you. Read the sentence carefully because you may need to add <u>s</u> or <u>es</u> to the vocabulary word.

Page 130: Use the information in *Global Warming* to answer the following questions. Answer each question in a complete sentence.

Page 131: Read the following sentences. For each sentence underline the subject once, draw a square around the action word (verb), draw a circle around the adverb, and put an x above the article (if there is an article). In these sentences the adverb modifies the verb by telling *how, when* or *where*. The three articles are *a, an*, and *the*. Remember to find the action word first and then the subject that is doing the action. The first one has been done for you. **Rewrite** the above five sentences adding *where* information or a *when* clause to each sentence. **Now** write five sentences of your own making sure each has an adverb to modify the verb, a verb, and a subject. Your sentence can also include an article.

Page 132: On this page each sentence needs a subject part, an action part, and a *when* clause. Read each sentence and then decide which part is missing. If the subject part is missing write S at the end of the sentence. If the action part is missing write V (for verb). If the *when* clause is missing write W. Then write in a word or words for the missing part. The first one has been done for you.

Lesson 20

Page 134: Alphabetize the English vocabulary words. To alphabetize, write all the <u>a</u> words first, then the <u>b</u>, then <u>c</u>, <u>d</u>, <u>e</u>, and so forth. If two words begin with the same letter, then look at the next letter and write the word which has the second letter closest to the beginning of the alphabet.

Page 135: Fill in each blank with a word from the vocabulary page. Use the Spanish word at the end of the sentence to help you. Read the sentence carefully because you may need to add <u>s</u> or <u>es</u> to the vocabulary word.

Page 137: Use the information in The *Arctic* to answer the following questions. Answer each question in a complete sentence.

Page 138: Use the words in the box to write the correct verb under each picture. **On** another piece of paper write a sentence with each word.

Page 139: Write the name of each picture in the correct category.

Índice

Index

Books Available From **FISHER HILL**
For Ages 10-Adult

ENGLISH READING COMPREHENSION FOR THE SPANISH SPEAKER Book 1, 2, 3, 4, & 5

ENGLISH READING AND SPELLING FOR THE SPANISH SPEAKER Books 1, 2, 3, 4, 5 & 6

ENGLISH for the SPANISH SPEAKER Books 1, 2, 3, 4 & Cassettes

SPANISH made FUN and EASY Books 1 & 2

HEALTH Easy to Read

UNITED STATES OF AMERICA Stories, Maps, Activities in Spanish and English Books 1, 2, 3, & 4

English Reading Comprehension for the Spanish Speaker Books 1, 2, 3, 4, & 5 contain twenty lessons to help Spanish-speaking students improve their English reading comprehension skills. Lessons include practice with vocabulary, visualization, fluency, phonology, and comprehension. Each lesson has an answer key. These are excellent books to use after completing *English Reading and Spelling for the Spanish Speaker Books 1, 2, 3, 4, & 5.* Price is $15.95, size is 8 1/2 x11 and each book is approximately 161 pages. Book 1 ISBN 978-1-878253-37-8, Book 2 ISBN 978-1-878253-43-9, Book 3 ISBN 978-1-878253-44-6, Book 4 ISBN 978-1-878253-47-7, Book 5 ISBN 978-1-878253-48-4

English Reading and Spelling for the Spanish Speaker Books 1, 2, 3, 4, 5 & 6 contain twenty lessons to help Spanish-speaking students learn to read and spell English. The books use a systematic approach in teaching the English speech sounds and other phonological skills. They also present basic sight words that are not phonetic. The word lists are in Spanish and English and all directions are in Spanish with English translations. Each book is $14.95 and approximately 142 pages. Book size is 8 1/2 x 11. Book 1 ISBN 978-1-878253-27-9, Book 2 ISBN 978-1-878253-25-5, Book 3 ISBN 978-1-878253-26-2, Book 4 ISBN 978-1-878253-29-3, Book 5 ISBN 978-1-878253-30-9, Book 6 ISBN 978-1-878253-35-4.

ENGLISH for the SPANISH SPEAKER Books 1, 2, 3, & 4 are English as a Second Language workbooks for ages 10 - adult. Each book is divided into eight lessons and is written in Spanish and English. Each lesson includes: vocabulary, a conversation, a story, four activity pages, an answer key, two dictionaries: English-Spanish and Spanish-English, a puzzle section, and an index. Each book is $12.95 and approximately 110 pages. Book size is 8 1/2 x 11. Book 1 ISBN 978-1-878253-07-1, Book 2 ISBN 978-1-878253-16-3, Book 3 ISBN 978-1-878253-17-0, Book 4 ISBN 978-1-878253-18-7; Book 1 Cassette ISBN 978-1-878253-21-7, Book 2 Cassette ISBN 978-1-878253-32-3, Book 3 Cassette ISBN 978-1-878253-33-0, Book 4 Cassette ISBN 978-1-878253-34-7.

SPANISH made FUN and EASY Books 1 & 2 are workbooks for ages 10 - adult. Each book includes stories, games, conversations, activity pages, vocabulary lists, dictionaries, and an index. The books are for beginning Spanish students; people who want to brush up on high school Spanish; or for Spanish speakers who want to learn how to read and write Spanish. Each book is $14.95 and 134 pages. Book size is 8 1/2 x 11. Book 1 ISBN 978-1-878253-42-2, Book 2 ISBN 978-1-878253-46-0.

HEALTH Easy to Read contains 21 easy to read stories. After each story is a vocabulary page, a grammar page, and a question and answer page. The stories are about changing people's life styles to reduce their risk of poor health and premature death. Book is $13.95 and has 118 pages. Book size is 8 1/2 x 11. ISBN 978-1-878253-41-5.

United STATES of America Stories, Maps, Activities in SPANISH and ENGLISH Books 1, 2, 3, & 4 are easy to read books about the United States of America for ages 10 - adult. Each state is presented by a story, map, and activities. Each book contains information for 12 to 13 states and has an answer key and index. The states are presented in alphabetical order. Book size is 8 1/2 x 11. Each book is $14.95 and approximately 140 pages.
Book 1 ISBN 978-1-878253-23-1 Alabama through Idaho
Book 2 ISBN 978-1-878253-11-8 Illinois through Missouri
Book 3 ISBN 978-1-878253-12-5 Montana through Pennsylvania
Book 4 ISBN 978-1-878253-13-2 Rhode Island through Wyoming

Toll Free Ordering
1-800-214-8110
Monday-Friday 8am-5pm
Central Standard Time

Order On-Line
www.Fisher-Hill.com

Fisher Hill

5267 Warner Ave., #166
Huntington Beach, CA 92649-4079
www.Fisher-Hill.com

Order by Fax
714-377-9495

Questions or Concerns
714-377-9353

Purchase Order Number: _____

Bill To:
Name: _____
Address: _____
City: _____ State _____ ZIP _____
Phone: _____

Ship To: (if different than billing address)
Name: _____
Address: _____
City: _____ State _____ ZiP _____
Phone: _____

QUANTITY	ISBN	BOOK TITLE	PRICE	AMOUNT
	37-8	English Reading Comprehension for the Spanish Speaker Book 1	$15.95	
	43-9	English Reading Comprehension for the Spanish Speaker Book 2	$15.95	
	44-6	English Reading Comprehension for the Spanish Speaker Book 3	$15.95	
	47-7	English Reading Comprehension for the Spanish Speaker Book 4	$15.95	
	48-4	English Reading Comprehension for the Spanish Speaker Book 5	$15.95	
	27-9	English Reading and Spelling for the Spanish Speaker Book 1	$14.95	
	25-5	English Reading and Spelling for the Spanish Speaker Book 2	$14.95	
	26-2	English Reading and Spelling for the Spanish Speaker Book 3	$14.95	
	29-3	English Reading and Spelling for the Spanish Speaker Book 4	$14.95	
	30-9	English Reading and Spelling for the Spanish Speaker Book 5	$14.95	
	35-4	English Reading and Spelling for the Spanish Speaker Book 6	$14.95	
	07-1	English For The Spanish Speaker Book 1	$12.95	
	21-7	English For The Spanish Speaker Book 1 Cassette	$10.95	
	20-0	English For The Spanish Speaker Book 1 and Cassette	$21.95	
	16-3	English For The Spanish Speaker Book 2	$12.95	
	32-3	English For The Spanish Speaker Book 2 Cassette	$10.95	
	38-5	English For The Spanish Speaker Book 2 and Cassette	$21.95	
	17-0	English For The Spanish Speaker Book 3	$12.95	
	33-0	English For The Spanish Speaker Book 3 Cassette	$10.95	
	39-2	English For The Spanish Speaker Book 3 and Cassette	$21.95	
	18-7	English For The Spanish Speaker Book 4	$12.95	
	34-7	English For The Spanish Speaker Book 4 Cassette	$10.95	
	40-8	English For The Spanish Speaker Book 4 and Cassette	$21.95	
	41-5	HEALTH Easy to Read	$13.95	
	23-1	USA Stories, Maps, Activities in Spanish & English Book 1	$14.95	
	11-8	USA Stories, Maps, Activities in Spanish & English Book 2	$14.95	
	12-5	USA Stories, Maps, Activities in Spanish & English Book 3	$14.95	
	13-2	USA Stories, Maps, Activities in Spanish & English Book 4	$14.95	
	42-2	SPANISH made FUN & EASY Book 1	$14.95	
	46-0	SPANISH made FUN & EASY Book 2	$14.95	
	MW920-7	Diccionario Español-Inglés	$6.50	
	MW852-1	Diccionario de Sinónimos y Antónimos en Inglés	$6.50	
	MW890-3	Juego de Diccionarios	$19.50	
	MW605-3	Dictionary of Basic English	$9.95	

Credit Card Information
Card Number: _____
Expiration Date: _____
Name: _____
Address: _____
City: _____ State _____ ZIP _____
Phone: _____

TOTAL _____

Add 7.75% for shipments to California addresses. SALES TAX _____

Add 10% of TOTAL for shipping. (Minimum $4.00) SHIPPING _____

PAYMENT _____

BALANCE DUE _____